DIVORCED CHRISTIANS
AND THE LOVE OF GOD

Paula Clifford is a Christian who is divorced, and
the mother of three children. She lives in Oxford
where she is a member of an Anglican church, and
lectures in French at the University besides working as a freelance writer and translator.

Divorced Christians and the Love of God

PAULA CLIFFORD

TRi∧NGLE

First published 1987
Triangle
SPCK
Holy Trinity Church
Marylebone Road
London NW1 4DU

British Library Cataloguing in Publication Data

Clifford, Paula
    Divorced Christians and the Love of God
    1. Divorce — Religious aspects —
    Christianity
    I. Title
    261.8'3589   BT707

    ISBN 0-281-04271-3

Typeset by Hart-Talbot Printers Ltd, Saffron Walden, Essex
Printed in Great Britain by
Hazell, Watson & Viney Limited
Member of the BPCC Group
Aylesbury, Bucks

Contents

Acknowledgements

Unless otherwise stated, Bible quotations are from the Holy Bible, New International Version. Copyright © 1973, 1978, 1984, International Bible Society.

Bible quotations marked RSV are from the Revised Standard Version of the Bible, copyrighted 1946, 1952, © 1971, 1973 by the Division of Christian Education of the National Council of the Churches of Christ in the USA, used by permission.

The quotation marked GNB is from the Good News Bible — Old Testament: Copyright © American Bible Society 1976.

The Collect from St Mary Magdalen is from the Alternative Service Book 1980, and this and the two other extracts from that book are reproduced with permission.

*Those who hope in the Lord
will renew their strength.*

Isaiah 40.31

Introduction

I am an incorrigible last-minute Christmas shopper. The first Christmas that I spent alone with my children after my marriage ended I had planned to make as normal as possible. So, true to form, on Christmas Eve I was in the toy department of a large store, with my three little believers in Father Christmas close beside me, when it suddenly dawned on me: I had forgotten the stocking fillers! Having sent the children off to look at toys at the far end of the department I began to feel rather like a shoplifter as I surreptitiously slid a succession of tiny items towards the cashier. I was absurdly cross with myself for not having realized that I would need a babysitter in order to carry out such a routine task, and it was a mistake I vowed never to make again.

That year was full of equally unforeseen situations. Some were sad, a few were funny and many were an unexpected source of blessing. Although I was not then very good at reading the Bible, I was much comforted and encouraged by Psalm 139: 'If I rise on the wings of the dawn, if I settle on the far side of the sea, even there your hand will guide me, your right hand will hold me fast' (Ps. 139.9-10).

This is a book for and about Christians whose marriages have ended in separation or divorce and for those who care for them. It is not autobiographical; I have learnt much from my own experience, but far more from other people. The first two chapters explore some of the emotions that accompany the end of a marriage, while subsequent chapters suggest some practical and positive ways forward. Each chapter ends with suggestions for Bible reading and prayer, which can be used alone or with someone else, and some books for further reading. A short appendix lists some useful addresses and sources of further information.

Although the particular question of the children of divorced parents has been constantly in my mind, I have not attempted to examine separately the problems presented for and by children. Indeed, it would need a separate book to do justice to the subject. On the other hand, I believe that the whole family is involved in the healing that God offers, and this belief underlies much of what is said in Part I.

I am much indebted to all those who have shared with me gladly and freely their experiences of separation and divorce, as well as those who have spoken to me about bereavement and singleness. If this was painful they did not show it but gave me much encouragement in writing this book.

I cannot begin to express adequately my gratitude to the many people who have offered me personal support and encouragement in all sorts of ways over the years. Many, although not all, of them are or have at some time been associated with St Andrews Church, Oxford or the Lee Abbey community in North Devon. This book is dedicated to them, with my love.

Oxford, 1986   Paula Clifford

PART I

Looking Inwards

1

Working through Emotions

There is nothing glamorous about divorce. It is only in Hollywood that marriages seem to come and go in glittering succession with flashing cameras and multi-million dollar settlements. And even there who knows what pain lies beneath the superficial splendour.

There is nothing routine or ordinary about divorce either. No matter how high the statistics show the divorce-rate to be, behind those figures there will always be pain, heartache, guilt and hardship. Quite simply, being separated or divorced is not a situation people would want to be in, given the choice. Even if marriage has come to spell misery to the couple concerned, and even if its end seems like a merciful release, the end when it does come nonetheless represents a shattering blow to the hopes once held and the love once shared.

The emotions which are part and parcel of marriage breakdown are many and complex, and they affect Christians and non-Christians alike. Being a Christian does not render you immune to them any more than it automatically saves you from the breakdown in the first place. All the pluses of the Christian life – faith, love, fellowship and so on – are counterbalanced by feelings of guilt at having somehow let down God and his people, and perhaps too by condemnation within the church. It is only recently that Christians have begun to acknowledge that divorce happens within their own ranks, and that it calls for special pastoral care, as do other matters of life and death, not least those to which some sort of social stigma is attached.

My starting point is the fact of separation or divorce, whichever may represent the end of a marriage for particular couples. I am not here concerned with ways of rescuing the marriage, nor with the tensions or difficulties within it. Instead I am beginning where so many Christian books on marriage stop, a notable exception being Wendy Green's excellent book, *The Christian and Divorce*[1]. My first concern, therefore, is to look at the very particular emotions generated by marriage breakdown and then to use these as a starting point for continuing in the Christian life and growing in it through them.

Identifying the Emotions

Feeling Different

It is hard to over-emphasize the intensity of the feeling of 'difference' experienced at the end of a marriage. A friend of mine was recently discomforted by a member of her congregation who was interrogating a young mother as to her husband's whereabouts, quite unaware that the couple had separated. 'I just wished she'd say outright that he'd gone,' said my embarrassed friend, failing to realize just how difficult, if not impossible, such a bald statement would have been for the girl to make.

A number of things lie behind this characteristic breakdown in communication. Above all, perhaps, it is the feeling that 'I am no longer as I was' or, more significantly, 'I am no longer what you expect me to be'. No one likes to feel different and for the Christian the sense of going contrary to the accepted – and 'right' – pattern is particularly acute. It is a sad paradox that when it comes to admitting failure life may be easier among non-Christian friends than among other Christians. Even so the feeling of being different is likely to persist, ranging from being merely embarrassing to all but intolerable, and this may well result in various forms of withdrawal.

It is inescapably true that Christians for the most part do not expect the marriages of their Christian friends to end; nor do they readily anticipate that newcomers to their fellowship may be divorced. Over the years one may learn to forestall the inevitable questions like 'Where is your wife?', 'What does your husband do?', but it is not easy if you are to avoid sounding unduly aggressive.

Perhaps only those who have been through the experience themselves can fully understand such feelings. For this reason I believe it is important that clergy and pastors should be aware of divorced Christians who are prepared to help care for others in this situation, even if the bulk of the counselling is done by someone else. If not, the feeling that no one understands can easily become overwhelming and it is but a short step to the conviction that God does not understand either.

When this happens it may be helpful to probe more deeply into the idea of 'difference'. If this is rooted in a sense of not coming up to expectations, a sense of failure, then there are plenty of examples in the Bible which illustrate God's love for such people. As Jesus himself said, when he had called Matthew, one of the hated tax-collectors, to be a disciple, 'It is not the healthy who need a doctor, but the sick . . . I have not come to call the righteous, but sinners' (Matt. 9.12 – 13). If, on the other hand, 'being different' stems especially from the awareness of having been let down and rejected, this is no more than the experience of Jesus. The prophecy of Isaiah 53, 'He was despised and rejected by men: a man of sorrows and acquainted with grief' (Isa. 53.3 RSV) finds poignant fulfilment in Peter's rejection of Jesus: 'He began to call down curses on himself, and he swore to them, "I don't know this man you're talking about" ' (Mark 14.71). Jesus knew all too well what it is like to be totally let down and abandoned by those closest to you. But in his case it was at the time when his need was greatest, in the face of death, and we can barely begin to imagine how great the emotional suffering, begun in Gethsemane, must have been.

For many divorced people it takes a long time to come to terms with being different. As grief begins to subside a restored sense of proportion tells them that they are not really being rejected by the rest of society. But trivial daily occurrences can easily revive a hurt which is perhaps never completely healed: glimpses of happy family groups, married couples showing their love for each other through no more than a look or gesture – all kinds of everyday situations. Occasions gladly attended in the past – school parents' evenings, office parties, church 'family days' – can all too easily prove an intolerable burden. They demand courage in the same way that, in other situations, being different in colour, size or ability from the social norm may also require courage and strength of character.

A former academic once told me that two things kept her going when her marriage ended. One was her work – she was a prolific writer – which occupied her mind and her time. The other was her local vicar's complete acceptance of her as a person. And this is just what is needed, the reassurance that you are accepted for yourself, as you are now. It does not imply that pains and problems are being swept under the carpet. Rather, it is the crucial first step in the whole process of healing, the rebuilding of the conviction that, whatever the circumstances, you are really no different from anyone else.

Feeling Guilty

The words 'sin' and 'guilt' are decidedly unfashionable. It is a bold evangelist who berates the unconverted for their sinfulness, and Christians themselves do not find the idea very palatable either. Some will say that this is a consequence of the permissive society. Whether or not this is true, it is certainly the case that our language has tended more and more to reserve the words 'guilt' and 'sin' for crimes carrying severe penalties in law. Nowadays, for example, Christians as well as non-Christians will talk about an unmarried couple 'living together' rather than 'living in sin', without necessarily condoning such a state of affairs.

One consequence of this is that many people find it quite

hard to understand what divorced people mean when they talk of an overwhelming sense of guilt. They will argue that someone who has been abandoned, for example, has not done anything wrong, and anyway the legal concept of 'guilty' and 'innocent' parties has long since been abolished. And yet of all the emotions that are bound up with the end of a marriage, the feeling of guilt can well be the most devastating and the most lasting.

There can be very few marriages in which one partner alone is wholly to blame for the break up, the exceptions being cases where factors such as character-changing illness may have intervened. To lay the blame fairly and squarely on one person can therefore have the effect of increasing the guilt felt by the other party, who knows that this is just not true. Moreover, those counselling the divorced need to recognize that this feeling of guilt may well be aggravated by depression and should be taken very seriously.

What is this guilt? Basically it is a sense of having let everyone down: other members of the family, friends, yourself and, perhaps worst of all, your children. The knowledge that your own actions have contributed to your children being deprived of one of their parents is very hard indeed to come to terms with. In addition, Christians will be all too conscious of having 'failed' God. The marriage vows taken before God have been broken; God, it seems, has been let down. Once reconciliation is no longer an option, it seems to me that the promises made to each other have been broken for good and no subsequent action (such as holding back from a second marriage) can alter that.

One thing, however, does change it all. Not only is God too great to be 'let down', but he is by nature a God of forgiveness who does not hold our failures against us:

> If you, O Lord, kept a record of sins,
> O Lord, who could stand?
> But with you there is forgiveness;
> therefore you are feared. (Ps. 130.3–4)

This is surely the great starting point for coping with the problem of guilt. Jesus forgave all who came to him in penitence and faith, and he died so that we too should enjoy that same forgiveness; that was the whole point of the Cross. The Letter to the Romans could never be called easy reading, but it is well worth reflecting on the great truths expressed in chapters 5 and 6, perhaps in a modern translation or with the help of a commentary. Paul writes there: 'Very rarely will anyone die for a righteous man . . . But God demonstrates his own love for us in this: While we were still sinners Christ died for us' (Rom. 5.7–8). And the result? 'Count yourselves dead to sin but alive to God in Christ Jesus' (Rom. 6.11). This new life in Christ does not, of course, render us immune to sin; but through Christ God forgives us. As St John puts it: 'If anybody does sin, we have one who speaks to the Father in our defence – Jesus Christ, the Righteous One. He is the atoning sacrifice for our sins, and not only for ours but also for the sins of the whole world' (1 John 2.1–2).

I have heard of several instances where clergy have reacted to the breakdown of a Christian marriage simply by telling those concerned to go to confession. In one such instance a wife was unable to promise to try to repair the marriage that had broken down 'irretrievably', and full absolution was withheld.

Now there are many Christians who will derive much comfort from confession, and not just those who are well accustomed to this particular tradition. There is also the danger, however, that this might constitute a kind of opting out. On the one hand confession may be the all-too-ready solution offered by a priest or pastor who is unable to cope with the care and counselling of the separated or divorced which ought in any case to accompany absolution. On the other hand the fact of having been to confession may lead people to feel that they should no longer feel or talk about guilt, and to suppress this and other emotions to detrimental effect.

Feeling guilty, then, is a strong emotion that needs to be faced up to. It is not necessarily more 'important' than rejection or loneliness, although it may appear so if confession is advocated to the exclusion of all else. But it is not an unnecessary emotion either, however an outsider may view the situation. It is something which should not be hidden or denied, for it is very real and a predictable response to what has happened. Until this is acknowledged, whether in the confessional, in private prayer or in conversation with friends, it cannot be brought to God for him to deal with.

When you are at peace with God, everything else becomes much easier. Inevitably there will still be the embarrassing conversations with friends and relatives, and of course there will still be sorrow at the thought of a child lacking a parent. Yet once you seek God's forgiveness you can be sure that his peace will take over and, however unlikely it may seem at the time, guilt will in the end be replaced by joy.

Feeling Lonely

Loneliness brings out the worst in all of us. If we stopped to consider why young people away from home fall in with the 'wrong set', would we not find again and again a longing for company – any sort of company: preferably people with whom they have something in common, if only an ill-defined sense of rebellion, and for whose companionship they are prepared to adopt whatever way of life may be the norm.

Many people who cannot come to terms with their own company, whatever their marital state, will resort to all kinds of devious means to avoid spending an evening on their own. Left to ourselves we can all too easily feel rejected, as well as bitter and angry with those who we feel have put us in this situation, angry with both man and God. The utterly destructive nature of such reactions is all too obvious.

Loneliness is an inevitable consequence of the end of a marriage. It may not come as suddenly and as shatteringly as it does in bereavement, and it may not take the same form of unending emptiness. But it does happen, whether or not there are children or other people in the house, and it has to be worked through. Whereas the bereaved may find some comfort in their memories, this is an escape which is denied to the divorced. In the light of later events even the happiest memories can be soured and again there is a very real risk of bitterness.

People seem to react to loneliness in two completely opposite ways. Some will withdraw completely into themselves, while others will opt for excessive activity. Both reactions are a form of escapism, either from society or from oneself; to find someone either at home every time you call or else always out, are both danger signals. Both reactions create a breakdown in communication, either because the person becomes too introverted to share his or her feelings or too extrovert to admit to them. Similarly, it seems to me that there are two complementary approaches to the problem of loneliness after divorce, which may be summed up as knowing yourself and knowing God.

The idea of 'knowing oneself' is one that I shall come back to several times in the chapters on 'New Directions'. R.E.O. White has rightly pointed out that being one in Christ does not mean being all alike. On the contrary, he writes, 'Personality differences are innate: which means that they are natural, inexplicable and unchangeable – even by religion'.[2] The implication of this is that no one can lay down precisely how each one of us would or should react in any given situation. There may (perhaps) be such a thing as a general 'Christian response' to particular problems, but the details of that response will be different for every Christian, depending on his or her personality.

It follows, then, that Christians will react emotionally in a variety of ways to the loss of a companion, without any

8

reactions being necessarily more, or less, 'Christian' than others. In coping with such a situation, therefore, self-knowledge is an important guideline for subsequent behaviour.

There are many people for whom being alone normally holds no fears. They may have interests, hobbies or talents which more than fill their time and which are satisfying in themselves. Others are able to relax on their own without the need for being constantly occupied; and there are others for whom music, reading or the companionship of a cat or dog may be enough to fill the void. On the other hand there are also people who either fear being alone and consequently will do anything to avoid it, or who when it happens fall into varying degrees of self-pity or depression.

Most of us no doubt react to being alone in different ways, depending on the particular situation. The prospect of a peaceful evening at home after a busy day may produce a positive reaction; but the knowledge that our friends are enjoying themselves at a party to which we have not been invited creates a totally different response.

Whatever these reactions may be, it is important that each individual recognizes them through examining his own personality. If, for instance, you are aware that a weekend spent alone is likely to lead to depression, you may want to plan to break the time up by contact with other people, however brief, rather than do all your socializing in one fell swoop on Friday night. In other words, make sure that there is always some respite from being alone to look forward to in the not too distant future, if that is what is best for you.

Knowing oneself is best done through honest examination, so as to arrive at an assessment that is neither too optimistic and self-deluding, nor too pessimistic and self-denigrating. It can be done alone or with a sympathetic friend, and may go a long way towards averting some of the trauma of separation.

The second factor which helps a Christian to cope with

being alone is an awareness of the nature of God as revealed in Jesus. I have already suggested that Jesus knew human loneliness all too well when he was abandoned by his friends after Gethsemane. This is akin to the loneliness experienced by men and women in many different places and times and for all kinds of reasons.

But Jesus suffered still more. On the cross he experienced loneliness pushed to its extreme: the feeling that God was no longer there with him. The writer of Psalm 22 conveys the agony of human loneliness in the opening verses:

> My God, my God, why have you forsaken me?
>> Why are you so far from saving me,
>>> so far from the words of my groaning?
> O my God, I cry out by day, but you do not answer,
>> by night, and am not silent.   (Ps.22.1–2)

Jesus knew the literal truth of being abandoned by God, but it is a truth that we need never know. As David Prior puts it, commenting on Matthew 27.46: 'The first implication for us of that experience by Jesus is that, however deeply we suffer, we are *not* forsaken by the Father. He is right there with us in our suffering to reveal himself as our Father.'[3]

We shall be looking again at this suffering in the next chapter, but for now it is sufficient to remember that Jesus knew as much about loneliness as any of us, and a great deal more besides. As a result, we ourselves need never be alone. In the words of Hans Küng, the crucified Christ 'sustains and supports man in the utmost peril, futility, triviality, abandonment, loneliness and emptiness: a God who identifies himself with man as one who is also affected'.[4]

Feeling Inadequate

There are times in all our lives when we do not feel up to the challenges of everyday living. We may have feelings of inadequacy at the prospect of a demanding job or a specific task; inadequacy at the idea of running a home, bringing up children, dealing with other people; inadequacy in the face of other people's expectations of us and in the face of God's love. We would not be human (or at least not very pleasant humans!) if we did not have some experiences like this from time to time.

However, just as separation or divorce entails experience of loneliness beyond that of temporary isolation which can happen to anyone, so too it can intensify 'normal' feelings of inadequacy to a very high degree. Marriage, after all, is the expression of the utmost confidence of one person in another. It is a source of wonder to couples in love that each partner can really feel the same way about the other, warts and all. Conversely, the end of a marriage seems like an expression of the complete and utter loss of that confidence in each other and the hurt goes far deeper than anything we may feel when, for example, a job we applied for is given to someone else.

It is not uncommon, therefore, to find someone whose marriage has ended suffering from a total loss of self-confidence. This may not be immediately obvious, for instance if the person concerned holds a prestigious or demanding job. But it is not the loss of confidence in one's professional skills and ability which is at issue. Rather it is the feeling of inadequacy *as a person* that can be over-whelming.

It is in personal relationships that this apparent inadequacy is most evident. After separation it is all but impossible for some people to imagine how anyone else could value them, not least anyone of the opposite sex. Single parents may have difficulty in imagining themselves as even beginning to function as mum as well as dad, or vice versa.

One of the most useful acts of friendship, therefore, can be helping to rebuild a person's self-confidence, even though it may not have been openly acknowledged that it has been lost. This might take the form of a special invitation, but might be no more than a complimentary remark. Gradually attention paid to the *person* will begin to bear fruit, for once the feeling of inadequacy begins to diminish, so too will other destructive emotions start to subside.

A divorced deaconess drew my attention to John 15. She explained how she had felt that she was a branch that had been cut off and discarded, but reading further, in Jesus's comments on the parable of the vine, she discovered: 'You did not choose me, but I chose you to go and bear fruit – fruit that will last' (John 15.16). It is not, therefore, for us to decide that we are inadequate and to be rejected. If God has chosen us how can we be inadequate as people? The answer is that we cannot, and although this is a fact which people who have been hurt may not be able to grasp all at once, it is the best possible basis for encouraging them back to confidence in their own worth and in God's love for them.

Working Through these Emotions

In the first part of this chapter I have tried to isolate a few of the emotions which are characteristically felt when a marriage ends, and in doing so I have offered some suggestions for beginning to come to terms with them. The crucial first step is actually to identify – or help someone else identify – what feelings are involved, and bound up with this is a need for honest self-appraisal. Now, having begun to appreciate the range of different feelings and emotional experiences underlying separation, the next stage is to work through them and beyond them, in a way that is both practical (in that it enables you or someone else to cope with day-to-day situations) and creative (enabling those experiences to be put to good use).

The traditional British reserve with its 'stiff upper lip' mentality is not an asset where emotions are concerned. Just as this may be a real obstacle to people who are trying to communicate their faith, so it is to many who might communicate their emotions. Yet if emotional problems are to be overcome they need first to be shared, and this is easier for some than for others. We are all familiar with the kind of person who will divulge every detail of their private lives to anyone who can be persuaded to listen. But such people are the exception rather than the rule, and the majority will need some encouragement to share their feelings, whether with others or with God, particularly when the 'guilt factor' is present. It may be helpful to consider briefly three ways of communicating emotions: with the professionals, with other Christians and with God.

Communicating with Professionals

More often than not, surely, divorce entails some form of illness suffered by one or both partners in the former marriage. Now one of the great advances in medicine in recent years is undoubtedly the recognition of depression and allied states as needing medical treatment, and not as something which can be 'snapped out of'. Yet it is said that many Christians are loath to accept this, believing instead that there must be something wrong with their spiritual life. According to John White both Christians and Jews view depression in spiritual terms as letting God down.[5] They are presumably even more likely to do this when, as we have seen, a feeling of guilt may have been one of the causes of the depression in the first place.

Not to seek medical help when it is freely available and clearly called for is simply to be perverse. It is not a sign of weakness or lack of faith; it is a sensible early step on the road to healing. The same applies to the many professional counselling services and voluntary organizations which offer help to those in various kinds of need. These will differ according to the part of the country in question, and all I want to do here is to mention in general terms three sources of help.

First, obvious as it may seem, there is the family doctor. If there is any possibility of marriage breakdown causing illness (of which insomnia may be the first sign), the surgery should be the first port of call. Never mind the press reports about the over-prescribing of tranquillizers or addiction to sleeping tablets; a GP's job is to assess and deal with the needs of his patients and we should be grateful for the God-given gifts of medical knowledge and skill. We should not reject treatment for emotional disorders any more than we would refuse medication for physical ones. It may be, of course, that there are good reasons for avoiding the doctor's surgery – if he or she is known to be unsympathetic to emotional problems, for example, or perhaps is treating the other marriage partner. In that case it is generally easy to change doctor and there is no question of having to explain one's action to the old one, as people sometimes imagine.

Secondly there are the professional counselling services. There are a growing number of counselling centres throughout the country, some of which include the word 'Christian' in their name, although this does not mean that they are closed to non-Christians. They are staffed by professional counsellors who are in consultation with a psychiatrist or doctor, and referral is generally done by GPs or hospitals, or, in the case of Christian centres, by parish priests as well.

Thirdly, there are the voluntary organizations such as the Samaritans, and I include them under the 'professional' label because they exist solely to communicate with those in distress. Contrary to popular belief the bulk of the Samaritans' work is not with the suicidal. Their function is to provide a listening ear at any hour of the day or night (their local branch number and/or address will be listed in the telephone directory) and to offer advice only if requested to do so. Although many of their volunteers are Christian they will not normally talk to clients in specifically Christian terms. There is the advantage of complete anonymity and the freedom to say what you like, how you like, to a sympathetic stranger.

Doctors, psychiarists, counsellers and volunteers have this in common, that they encourage communication. Since there is no emotional involvement with them many people welcome the chance to talk about their problems without a personal relationship with the listener getting in the way.

Communicating with other Christians

Communicating with the professionals is relatively easy; firstly because they are trained to probe the physical or psychological maladies of others, and secondly because a doctor-patient relationship, say, depends on certain expectations: to get cured the patient has to tell the doctor what his symptoms are as fully as possible, and he will usually do so.

Communicating with other Christians can be much harder. For the most part they are not professionals, and therefore their own hang-ups may have to be taken into account as well. Yet solidarity with those who are suffering is part of our Christian calling, and natural reticence on the part of either the sufferer or the comforter, or both, has to be set aside. David Prior draws attention to 2 Corinthians 1.4: '[God] comforts us in all our troubles, so that we can comfort those in any trouble with the comfort we ourselves have received from God', and he goes on to talk about a 'rhythm' of suffering and comfort.[6] The Christian ideal, therefore, is neither to withhold comfort nor to reject it.

Perhaps the most telling thing about this verse from 2 Corinthians is the recognition of an affinity between those who are in trouble and those who have themselves experienced suffering. The Christians who are best placed to help the divorced, therefore, are those who have suffered in some way, whether through divorce themselves, or through bereavement, sickness or some other situation that may give rise to similar emotional difficulties.

It is unfortunate that while there is plenty of resource material to help those involved in caring for the bereaved, there is little help available for those who counsel the divorced. If anything, their need is greater. Unlike professional counsellors, ordinary Christians may have to set aside their own, possibly strong, views on the marriage breakdown before they can begin to help. Alternatively, they may have led more sheltered lives than non-Christians in this respect and may not previously have encountered anyone whose marriage has broken up. In such cases it is fear or embarrassment that has to be overcome before any effective help can be given.

It is evident that the ideal of comfort has all too often broken down. Swihart and Brigham observe: 'The church community needs to offer forgiveness, be supportive and bring healing. Yet often it is the last place Christians turn for support when they are divorced or separating.'⁷ Nonetheless it is the right of any Christian to seek and expect such support from his or her fellow Christians. In many churches this happens on a formal basis, for example through a system of lay pastors, and on an informal basis as well, as members of the community spontaneously offer care to one another.

Perhaps because of the embarrassment which impedes communication some Christians may well find comfort outside their own churches, either through chance encounters with other Christians, or by attending other churches, or through some more structured Christian event. For example there is now a regular annual holiday week for single parents and their children at the Lee Abbey holiday and conference centre in North Devon, and this has been the source of spiritual blessing to many. Some Christians may want to consider retreats at religious communities, or may seek help in a church or fellowship where they do not feel under any pressure.

Why bother? If someone feels able to get by on sleeping tablets, a psychiatrist or his own spiritual resources, why should he risk further hurt from the church community? The answer is, because it is God's will for his people. It is only by coming closer to one another that we can come closer to God. This applies to sufferers and comforters alike, but to the benefit of both. 'Our hope for you is firm', wrote St Paul, 'because we know that just as you share in our sufferings, so also you share in our comfort' (2 Cor. 1.7).

Communicating with God

If communicating with professionals comes at one end of a sliding scale between easy and difficult, and communicating with other Christians is around the middle, then communicating with God must surely seem to be placed at the end of extreme difficulty. After all, separation and divorce can all too easily be the crisis points at which people turn away from God and the Church. In moments of despair we become incapable of communicating with God, and through our self-absorption we prevent him from speaking to us. How can the lines be reopened?

I recently heard a retired vicar speak of the conversion of a young sailor during the Second World War. When the lad was asked what difference it had made to his life he replied: 'I don't say my prayers any more; I talk to God.' It seems to me that this simple statement, while expressing the reality of a Christian's relationship with God, also hints at the hope which is inherent in any form of communication with him. It does not matter that feelings of guilt or despair prevent us from repeating set prayers or familiar formulae. God keeps the lines of communication open for us, even though all he may hear from us are our 'groans' and 'sighing'. In the words of Job, 'sighing comes to me instead of food; my groans pour out like water' (Job 3.24). The publisher Edward England came to a similar conclusion following the death of his first wife: 'All my life I had thought I had to tell [God] of my concerns, to spell them out, to daily ask for protection for those I loved. In my grief I accepted that he knew that there was no necessity to share verbally all the detail, that he came to me because I hurt rather than because of what I said.'[8]

The experience of marriage breakdown, as we have already seen, almost inevitably arouses feelings of inadequacy. It is hard, and at times impossible, to see the hand of God in it. And yet, as Jim Packer points out, God's purpose of drawing us ever closer to himself is achieved 'not by protecting us from burdensome and frustrating circumstances, nor yet by shielding us from troubles created by our own temperament and psychology; but rather by exposing us to all these things, so as to overwhelm us with a sense of our own inadequacy, and to drive us to cling to him more closely'.[9]

Here then are two good grounds for reassurance whenever we feel inadequate before God and unable to pray because of pain or misery. The first reason is that God comes to us when we are incapable of coming to him, and the second is that this leads us in our turn to draw closer to him in and through our weakness.

It is often very moving to pray with people who are in this position, but it is a form of ministry which also demands a certain amount of tact. On the one hand it is helpful to try to articulate before God something of what you know the other person to be suffering, but not, on the other hand, to be so articulate as to heighten any sense of spiritual inadequacy on their part. Most people will appreciate a visitor who is able to pray briefly and naturally with them in this way; alternatively, the promise to remember the family or

18

individual in prayer (so long as it is kept) is just as valuable.

In communicating with God the Bible is our greatest asset. After all, what better basis for prayer than Scripture itself. Edward England says: 'With David I confess my sin . . . ; with Isaiah I hear the call of God to serve; with Peter I make the great confession: Jesus is God; with the Apostle Paul I name him Lord.'[10] Primarily, though, it is God who through Scripture is communicating with us, and the question may well be, where to start?

Some Christians will have the Bible at their fingertips and appear to know exactly where to turn for passages of hope, comfort or whatever. But not even the most dedicated biblical scholar has all the answers. Sharing a single verse with someone who has never had occasion to apply it to his or her own suffering may be helping that person to re-establish communication with God.

Others may feel more inadequate than ever. Not only have they failed and are unable to pray about it, but they do not know where to look in the Bible for the message they have been told is there. Most of us have our favourite passages to recommend in such situations, but again there are pitfalls. It will not, for example be helpful to list the teachings on marriage and divorce; nor would I personally recommend (as I have heard some do) reading the Book of Job right through – unless you have a particular interest in literary structure! The Psalms would be one place to start, but it is always good to have a clear idea as to which ones (or which parts) to recommend.

From what I have said above it should be clear that in helping divorced or separated people re-establish communication with God other Christians also have an important role to play. Naturally the extent of their involvement will vary but it is something which should not be feared on either side.

A third channel of communication with God, besides prayer and Scripture, is one in which other Christians are necessarily involved, that is through the ministry of healing. From James 5 we understand that the sick are entitled to call the 'elders of the church' (e.g. the Parochial Church Council, house-group leaders, the spiritually mature) to pray over them and anoint them in the name of the Lord. The sick will be healed, sins will be forgiven. Furthermore, we are urged to minister in this way to one another: 'Confess your sins to each other and pray for each other so that you may be healed. The prayer of a righteous man is powerful and effective' (Jas. 5.16).

More and more churches are now taking seriously this exhortation and its attendant promise. Prayer for the sick and the laying on of hands happens most frequently – and perhaps most appropriately – within the context of a Communion service, but some churches will also have their own healing groups or special healing services. If this practice is unfamiliar to them, divorced Christians may well need some reassurance as to the suitability of this ministry for them and the assurance of confidentiality.

It is hard to convey in words the very moving experience of having a congregation in prayer for you, while perhaps knowing nothing at all about you, and of having the leaders lay their hands upon you and pray very simply for you and your needs in the terms you have outlined to them. Such ministry can be exercised in a church, in a private living room, or wherever and whenever the gift of healing is sought. As to the result, all pastors have their own stories of dramatic healings. But it is not appropriate that all prayer should be answered dramatically. For many, the laying on of hands will be an event which sustains and encourages, which, along with other forms of ministry, helps bring about a gradual process of rehabilitation and, above all, brings us closer to God.

In this chapter I have attempted to spell out some of the emotions associated with divorce, to help those for whom this is not within their experience and to try to reassure those for whom it is. I have also tried to indicate something of the value of working through these emotions with the help of others. It is only when these feelings have been laid bare that the healing process can begin. And it is only when suffering starts to recede that we can appreciate how through it God has drawn closer and revealed more of himself to us. It is this paradoxical 'privilege' of suffering that will occupy the next chapter.

FOR BIBLE READING AND MEDITATION

Isaiah perceived two strands to God's love for the people of Israel; it was an *active* love in that he got them out of hardship and trouble, and it was a *compassionate* love, for he shared their distress: 'In all their affliction he was afflicted, and the angel of his presence saved them; in his love and in his pity he redeemed them; he lifted them up and carried them all the days of old' (Isa. 63.9 RSV). This is the essence of God's nature: to be alongside us in our suffering and, as soon as we ask him, to act in our lives.

Read Psalm 25:

To you, O Lord, I lift up my soul;
   in you I trust, O my God.
Do not let me be put to shame,
   nor let my enemies triumph over me.
No one whose hope is in you
   will ever be put to shame,
but they will be put to shame
   who are treacherous without excuse.

Show me your ways, O Lord,
   teach me your paths;
   guide me in your truth and teach me,
   for you are God my Saviour,
   and my hope is in you all day long.

Remember, O Lord, your great mercy and love,
   for they are from of old.
Remember not the sins of my youth
   and my rebellious ways;
according to your love remember me,
   for you are good, O Lord.

Good and upright is the Lord;
   therefore he instructs sinners in his ways.
He guides the humble in what is right
   and teaches them his way.
All the ways of the Lord are loving and faithful
   for those who keep the demands of his covenant.
For the sake of your name, O Lord,
   forgive my iniquity, though it is great.
Who, then, is the man that fears the Lord?
   He will instruct him in the way chosen for him.
He will spend his days in prosperity,
   and his descendants will inherit the land.
The Lord confides in those who fear him;
   he makes his covenant known to them.
My eyes are ever on the Lord,
   for only he will release my feet from the snare.

Turn to me and be gracious to me,
   for I am lonely and afflicted.
The troubles of my heart have multiplied;
   free me from my anguish.
Look upon my affliction and my distress
   and take away all my sins.
See how my enemies have increased
   and how fiercely they hate me!
Guard my life and rescue me;
   let me not be put to shame,
   for I take refuge in you.
May integrity and uprightness protect me,
   because my hope is in you.

Redeem Israel, O God,
from all their troubles!

In this Psalm the writer affirms his faith in God and prays
for God's help and guidance in his own life. Notice how he
presents his personal situation in very general terms; consequently his guilt and loneliness become an expression of
ours. A great source of comfort for the Psalmist and for us is
remembering how God has acted on human lives in the past,
revealing always (in the words of the RSV) that 'all the paths
of the Lord are steadfast love and faithfulness'.

The Psalm begins with the assurance that God honours
our trust and will never let us down. Furthermore God does
not leave us on our own to struggle as best we can along the
way he wants us to go. He is ready to teach us the right way
and to guide our every step. If you have ever helped a small
child learning to walk you will understand something of the
tenderness and protectiveness which God shows to us, and
of our own weakness, inarticulateness and dependence on
him.

It is good, in the midst of despair, to reflect on the personal nature of God and to be reassured of his unfailing
mercy and love for each one of us. Although it hurts when
we feel rejected by other people, what really matters is that
God will not reject us. Because he, the best protector of all, is
prepared to guide us forward, we can be sure that ultimately
we will leave our unhappiness and turmoil behind, and
through that we will learn to love and serve him better.

We thank you, dear Lord, for the steadfast love you
have shown throughout history to all those who trusted
you, and for the assurance that you will keep us safe in the
midst of trouble. Thank you that when no one understands, you understand; when no one seems to care, you
care. We pray, Lord, that you will ease the burden of our
guilt, loneliness and despair; make our hearts ready to

receive you and teach us to follow wherever you will lead us. For the love of our Saviour Jesus Christ, who gave even his life for us. Amen.

Suggestions for further reading
Wendy Green's *The Christian and Divorce* (Mowbray 1981) still seems to me to be the best on the subject. On the emotional problems considered in this chapter, a sensible and readable treatment of depression is Martha Maughon's *Why am I Crying?* (Marshall 1983). A perceptive account of loneliness is contained in Roy Trevivian's, *So You're Lonely* (Fount Paperbacks 1978). For times when communication with God seems difficult there are many good things in *My Path of Prayer* edited by D. Hanes (Worthing 1981).

References

1 Mowbray 1981.
2 R.E.O. White, *A Guide to Pastoral Care* (Pickering & Inglis 1976), p.298.
3 D. Prior, *The Suffering and the Glory* (Hodder 1985), p.17.
4 H. Küng, *On Being a Christian* (Fount Paperbacks 1978), p.572.
5 J. White, *The Masks of Melancholy* (IVP 1982).
6 *The Suffering and the Glory,* p.23.
7 J.J. Swihart and S.L. Brigham *Helping Children of Divorce* (Scripture Union 1984), p.34.
8 In D. Hanes (ed.), *My Path of Prayer* (Henry Walter, Worthing, 1981), p.32.
9 J.I. Packer, *Knowing God* (Hodder 1973), p.281.
10 *My Path of Prayer,* p.39.

2

The Privilege of Suffering

Why Me?

The cry of a soul in despair, the cry of desolation is 'why?' When it is impossible for us to articulate our grief, 'why' is the one word that comes readily to our lips.

This cry that springs from the deepest human need abounds in Scripture. 'Why did I not perish at birth . . . ?' sums up the despair of Job (Job 3.11). 'Why, O Lord, do you stand far off? Why do you hide yourself in times of trouble?' cries the Psalmist (Ps. 10.1); 'How long, O lord? Will you forget me for ever?' (Ps. 13.1). This 'why?', this 'how long?' is not asking for a lecture on the purpose of suffering. It is much more basic than that: a desperate appeal for help and love in the face of human inadequacy. It is the cry of even the most self-sufficient, and it is the cry of Christians who are not so much questioning God's purposes as expressing their own helplessness.

It is interesting that the Bible gives us an answer on two levels. In the Psalms we find the necessary reassurance that God cares: 'You hear, O Lord, the desire of the afflicted; you encourage them, and you listen to their cry . . . ' (Ps. 10.17). The Book of Job, on the other hand, provides the answer to the serious questioning of God's plan for us: 'Where were you when I laid the earth's foundation? Tell me, if you understand' (Job 38.4), to which in the end Job can only reply: 'I know that you can do all things; no plan of yours can be thwarted' (Job 42.2).

To this basic question 'Why me?', then, the Bible not only offers a twofold answer, but it also recognizes the validity of such a question in the first place. 'Why should my marriage have broken down and not that of my neighbour?' does not receive a direct answer, but the question itself is not condemned. It is the means by which we are reassured of God's love for us and of his controlling hand in our lives. So it is not a question to be ashamed of, or swept aside; it deserves the answer that God will give.

This is not to say that we can expect to be given special insight into God's purpose. Yet it is precisely in the intimacy of our own lives – in the fullest possible knowledge of all the circumstances – that we can appreciate to a very small degree something of the way in which God works. But even that is usually glimpsed only in retrospect. And once we move away from ourselves, to look, for example, at infant victims of famine or violence, and contemplate the vast panorama of human suffering, then we understand nothing.

It is in our own personal suffering, whatever its nature and its cause, that we can find God if we choose to look for him. This simple fact should not be obscured by guilt on the one hand and a stubborn lack of forgiveness on the other. If this happens then the privileged position of the sufferer is jeopardized.

What Privilege?

When we are in pain all our defences are down. It does not matter whether or not that pain is of our own causing, nor whether it is mental, physical or spiritual. Some people will hold out against it more resolutely than others. I heard, for example, of a young Christian girl who, after her husband left her, objected to people asking her how she was. 'I'm happy, I feel all right,' she claimed. It was only when she stopped trying to fool herself as well as other people that she could start to see some kind of point to her suffering and allow God to come close to her.

Suffering offers an opportunity for us to stop pretending and to open ourselves to God. This is the first reason why it can be called a privilege. In times of trouble God is on our side against all the odds, as his ancient promise reminds us: 'When you pass through the rivers, they will not sweep over you. When you walk through the fire, you will not be burned' (Isa. 43.2). This is the promise which is restated by Jesus: 'In this world you will have trouble. But take heart! I have overcome the world' (John 16.33). Because Jesus took all our suffering upon himself on the cross we can align ourselves with him against the world; that is our privilege if we care to use it.

Many, if not most, Christians can testify to their own experiences of drawing close to God in suffering. What I want to stress is that the circumstances of that suffering are immaterial. We may be lying in a hospital bed, mourning a loved one, or grieving over our own mistakes. There is no such thing as 'respectable' suffering. God will use our pain, no matter where it comes from, to reveal more of himself to us, if we will let him.

God's presence with us in suffering has a dual purpose. First, clearly, it is for our comfort and ressurance. But, secondly, God's presence is a dynamic one that not only comforts us but gives us strength for what lies ahead. For we can be sure that when we allow God to come so close that he takes control of our lives, then the real spiritual battle against the world is only just beginning.

The Bible gives us many illustrations of this. In Mark's account of the Transfiguration, God's revelation of himself to Jesus and the three disciples is followed immediately by an encounter with evil (Mark 9.14ff.), and Jesus once more tells his uncomprehending followers of the way of suffering that lies ahead (Mark 9.31). Similarly, in the Old Testament, God calls his prophets and reveals himself to them, only to give them messages whose proclamation will inevitably bring them unpopularity and personal suffering. We have only to look at the life of Moses to see this pattern exemplified again and again.

Suffering, therefore, *is* a privilege, but not in the sense that anything has to be earned. God's comfort is freely given to anyone who seeks it. But this comfort brings with it a challenge to future action for which we are built up and it enables us to move forward in new directions in his strength.

My second reason for using the word 'privilege' is because we not only come nearer to God in suffering but through it also we are alerted to the suffering of others. The closer we come to the heart of God, the closer we also come to all the sufferings of his children in which he shares. This is another aspect of the challenge of God's presence with us as we are compelled to try in some small and almost insignificant way to alleviate some of the pain around us. It is also God's will for us, as Paul suggests in his description of the Body of Christ: 'If one part suffers, every part suffers with it; if one part is honoured, every part rejoices with it. Now you are the body of Christ, and each one of you is a part of it' (1 Cor. 12.26–7).

Two Witnesses

Karen suffers from manic depression, which first struck her after the birth of her first child. When she and her husband decided on another baby it was in the full knowledge that her depression would probably recur. It did, and she suffered from it for many years afterwards. During this time, which involved periods in a psychiatric hospital, her marriage gradually disintegrated. Her husband, left to cope with two young children, found himself a girlfriend. Meanwhile Karen became a Christian.

Throughout the divorce that ensued Karen needed much support from her Christian friends. Partly through this, but more specifically through her own encounter with God in her suffering, she began to thank God for both her mental

28

illness and her emotional pain. As she rejoiced in his love for her she began to tell others about what had happened to her.

Today Karen is still liable to attacks of depression and is still quite dependent on other people when she finds it hard to cope. Nonetheless she has come to realize her own limitations and within these limits has devoted much time and energy to setting up a support group for other depressives. Through the heightened awareness of suffering brought about by her own illness she has developed her own role in the community, which involves caring for others in a similar situation and an effective style of simple evangelism and witness.

Harry, on the other hand, is a widower. His wife became a Christian only weeks before she died of cancer. Harry's testimony is of the change this brought to his wife who was able to embrace death without the fear that had beset her until then. Despite his own grief and loneliness Harry can see God's purposes being worked out through all the pain and suffering. He is now exercising a healing ministry and developing an unmistakable gift for evangelism.

There is the same clear message in both these testimonies, that God uses our suffering. Yet it would be quite wrong to pretend that either Karen or Harry recognized this at the time when their suffering was greatest; to them it was evident only in retrospect. For outsiders, however, it is different; the way in which Christians cope with suffering often, in the eyes of others, bears eloquent testimony to God's presence with them, although they may be quite unaware of such witness at the time.

It is not until the immediate pain is dulled somewhat that we become aware of what has happened. C.S. Lewis described his sorrow after the death of his wife not as a state, but a process: 'It keeps on changing like a winding road with quite a new landscape at each bend.'[1] One of these landscapes is when we come to recognize God's controlling presence, whatever our particular burden of suffering.

As we have seen, one way in which God uses suffering may become apparent only when we stand back and look objectively at the pattern our lives have followed. Another way in which he uses it is to make clear to us certain truths about himself, and these we can perceive more readily in the midst of pain. I should like to mention just three such aspects of God in relation to marriage breakdown in particular: God understands, God shares our suffering, God is in control.

God understands. From my own experience I am led to conclude that divorced people can be extremely perverse! I find within myself, for example, an obstinate sort of confusion as regards my present status. I want people to know my position, but I do not want to have to tell them; on the other hand I am inclined to be resentful if someone else tells them for me! Similarly, I resent it if anyone inquires after my children in such a way as to imply that there is anything different about them; and I am equally disgruntled if my responsibilities as a mother are not acknowledged. Other people may experience other conflicts, such as being torn between being single and being married. In short, we cannot understand ourselves and we are unable to imagine how anyone else could understand us. All too readily we forget that God can and does understand: 'For you created my inmost being; you knit me together in my mother's womb' (Ps. 139.13).

It is tempting to open the Bible and come to the hasty conclusion that because Jesus lived a blameless human life or because he was not married, God cannot understand the problems of guilt or marriage breakdown. To do this is to devalue the whole sacrifice of the incarnation and the cross. In one form or another Jesus experienced every aspect of suffering; he learned more than we could ever know about temptation and the power of evil.

The consequence is that our God is supremely compassionate and forgiving, having experienced our weakness for himself. Jesus wept when his friend died; he was rejected by his family and friends; he was betrayed by those he trusted; and he suffered every kind of human injustice and torment in the events surrounding his crucifixion. In the light of all this, can we really pretend that God does not understand?

God understands more than just our particular situation. In Jesus as well we see our own vulnerability. We cannot live lives of any purpose by shutting ourselves off from the world in a sort of sterile bubble, any more than Jesus could. We cannot protect ourselves from hurt by not engaging in human relationships: this is not the example of Jesus. Like him we have to take the risk, and accept that God will help us bear the pain and rejection that may ensue. In order to make disciples Jesus had to accept the possibility that one of them might turn against him. In order to preach the word of God he had to risk the condemnation of the religious authorities. Every part of Jesus's earthly ministry involved some form of hurt, so who better to understand our vulnerability?

To sum up, God understands our complexity and irrationality because he created us. And he understands our weakness and our suffering, whatever it may be, because wherever we go Jesus has been there before us.

God shares our suffering. It is part of the privilege of suffering that God suffers with us. We are not expected to rise stoically above it, to set our minds on higher things and pretend that the pain is no longer there. God comes down to our level and is there with us.

There are many instances in the Bible where God's suffering alongside his creatures is depicted. Charles Ohlrich in his book *The Suffering God* explores this facet of God's nature in a way that is both illuminating and reassuring:

31

According to the Bible the peace which God gives is not a freedom from the storms of life, but a mysterious strength and comfort amid the storms; not the removal of pain, but the bestowal of a precious gift. The gift is God himself, the comforter, the one who 'stands along-side us'.[2]

There will, naturally, be times when the pain is too great for such a message to meet with anything other than uncomprehending bewilderment. That does not matter; rather like a friend or relative maintaining a silent vigil at the bedside of a loved one, so God waits with us, offering us his unsought presence and strength, for, in Ohlrich's words again, 'through Christ God put to death the worst of agonies – our feeling of abandonment'.[3]

When divorce happens the only truly innocent parties are children, and whether they become fatherless or motherless they suffer. Not only do they suffer in the sense of being disadvantaged; their emotional suffering can be extremely complex – feelings of loss, of guilt (arising from the fear that they have in some way caused their parents' separation) and of rejection, to name but three possibilities. Here we have the reassurance that the God who suffers cares especially for the weak. God, through Jeremiah, promised Edom: 'Leave your orphans; I will protect their lives. Your widows too can trust in me' (Jer. 49.11) and the Psalmist acknowledges this: 'You, O God, do see trouble and grief; you consider it to take it in hand. The victim commits himself to you; you are the helper of the fatherless' (Ps. 10.14).

Only God can really see the world from the child's perspective and understand it. The amazing resilience of so many children of separated parents is a sure testimony to God's protecting love at work in their lives. However deep the guilt and grief that parents may feel at having put a child in this position, they and those around them should not lose sight of God's special love for these little ones and should not cease to invoke it.

God does not, however, protect the weak in order that the strong may be relieved of their responsibilities. His presence will also strengthen and build up temporarily weakened parents and he does not fail to answer their prayer for strength to support their children.

This plea that God's particular love for children in painful situations should be recognized is not directed solely at parents. A recent book on the children of divorced parents contains the sad comment: 'Children in the Church often experience a subtle condemnation from church members if their parents are divorced.'⁴ Nothing could be more contrary to the will of God as it is reflected both in the Old Testament promises of protection and in the words of Jesus in the New Testament: 'Whoever welcomes a little child like this in my name welcomes me' (Matt. 18.5) and further, '... your Father in heaven is not willing that any of these little ones should be lost' (Matt. 18.14).

God, then, protects the weak in their suffering. For those unable to fend for themselves that protection is absolute. But God also gives us new strength so that we can both grow through our suffering and in turn offer strength and protection to those dependent on us.

I will sing of your strength,
   in the morning I will sing of your love;
for you are my fortress,
   my refuge in times of trouble.
O my Strength, I sing praise to you;
   you, O God, are my fortress, my loving God.

(Ps. 59.16–17)

God is in control. We have seen how God's involvement in our suffering is a very positive thing: it is life-restoring and strengthening, and it brings us to a deeper understanding of him. This leads on to the third divine characteristic which I would like to stress here, namely that God is in control.

While the ultimate reason for our suffering remains hidden from us, we can nonetheless come in due course to appreciate God's hand guiding us through it. Under his guidance we can come to understand more of the nature of our suffering and its function in our lives.

Suffering, mercifully, is not static: it contains within it both change and progression. Hans Küng describes it as 'a mode of coming to be',[5] the creative realization of our own humanity. I have already mentioned C.S. Lewis's view of bereavement as an ever-changing sorrow. Elsewhere the same author also finds in suffering a gradual approach to God: 'We shall draw nearer to God, not by trying to avoid the suffering inherent in all loves, but by accepting them and offering them to Him.'[6]

God is in control, then, as to these varying forms of suffering and the intensity of it. Paul's comment on temptation applies equally well here: 'God is faithful; he will not let you be tempted beyond what you can bear. But when you are tempted, he will also provide a way out so that you can stand up under it' (1 Cor. 10.13). The implication of this is that wherever God is in control there is hope; not necessarily the hope of an instant cure, but the promise of support and change.

This is just as valid in divorce as in bereavement. Slowly but surely God will teach us dependence on him in place of another person. So Karen speaks of learning to depend on God for absolutely everything in her life, from caring for the children to paying the gas bill, and from guiding her to new friends and fellowship to teaching her to become an evangelist.

God is in control not only here and now but in the future as well. Whatever the form of our suffering, we have to learn to cope with one day at a time, turning over each new situation to God as it arises. Then gradually we learn to apply our experience of his control in the present to our future. When the outlook seems bleak, when there even

34

appears to be no future, it is supremely reassuring to know that God has a future for us in a way that we cannot begin to imagine.

Finally, God is in control so completely that in the end we can see how he uses suffering to teach us more about ourselves and other people. He not only shows us our weaknesses but helps us to overcome them, and, incredible as it may sound, we learn to use our suffering for ourselves. Hans Küng defines this utilization of suffering as the 'positive, active acceptance and integration of suffering within the total meaning of life'. He goes on: 'Countless people . . . transformed their lives and acquired a new personal quality: through suffering became more mature, more experienced, more modest, more genuinely humble, more open for others – in a word, more human.'[7]

Through the suffering of divorce, then, as through any other form of pain, we can if we wish learn much more about humility, love and service. We can learn more about ourselves, other people and God: that is the real privilege of suffering.

Learning to Share

One of the lessons of suffering, as we have seen, is a new dependence on God. This entails, for the most part, a greater sharing of our lives with him than may have been the case in the past. However, along with this, I believe, go two other forms of sharing. The first is sharing with others the responsibilities, decisions, joys and sorrows previously shared only within the marriage relationship. The second is learning to share the sufferings of others as a result of one's own experience.

Individuals will differ in the degree to which they will need to develop the first kind of sharing. For example, someone who is well used to handling bills, income tax, mortgage repayments and so on is not suddenly going to seek someone else's assistance with them. Nonetheless I believe that it is important for a divorced or separated person to be sufficiently open to others to share problems such as these should the need arise. If not, there is a risk of a kind of dogged self-sufficiency which all too easily impedes the natural healing process. Furthermore, this is particularly vital where children are concerned.

Despite certain minority views in today's secular society, children were not meant to be raised by one parent alone, as the marriage service clearly states. Even where close contact is maintained with the absent parent, the person responsible for the day-to-day care of children will do well to share this with others, whether in seeking practical help, advice, or just encouragement and another adult for the children to relate to.

Encouragement is vital. We all think we have the best ideas about bringing up children and are very ready to criticize families who follow a different pattern from our own. Single-parent families inevitably start at a disadvantage in this respect, and critical eyes are rarely far away. It follows, then, that single parents are likely to need considerable encouragement just in their general way of life, before the contentious issues such as schools, discipline or pocket money even come into it.

Sharing like this often involves a learning process, not least on the part of the outsider. Criticism, for example, is not at all helpful unless it is accompanied by some constructive suggestion for improvement, just as it normally is within the family circle. You do not criticize the way your daughter dresses if you do not give her any guidance as to what suits her, or if her allowance is too small to enable her to replace laddered tights. Unfortunately it is all too easy for outsiders to do just this, which cannot fail to inhibit any desire for sharing on the part of the person under attack.

People cannot be forced to share matters they prefer to keep to themselves. Yet a little gentle encouragement, or simply the absence of criticism, will go a long way towards helping them to do so if they need to. My own family is particularly fortunate in the love and friendship offered by 'normal' Christian families. One such family has never commented adversely on details of our lifestyle but has offered encouragement just through a few approving comments which related almost uncannily to areas where I have been uncertain. A simple remark along the lines of 'It's nice to see the children doing such and such' is marvellous reassurance that you were right to let them do it in the first place.

Sharing concerns like this, and accepting that sharing, is surely in line with Paul's exhortations in Romans 12: 'Be devoted to one another in brotherly love . . . Be joyful in hope, patient in affliction, faithful in prayer. Share with God's people who are in need. Practise hospitality' (Rom. 12.10–13). Sadly, however, that stiff upper lip all too often prevents us from doing this as a normal part of our everyday lives. Yet it is of inestimable value when a relationship that has hitherto provided that devotion and sharing has broken down.

Seeking or giving advice on various domestic problems is an active, practical form of sharing. The other form that I have suggested is rather more passive and emotional. This is enabling others to share their suffering with you because they recognize, however dimly, that you have also suffered and they feel you might understand. This is a further privilege of suffering. Indeed, being able to help other people in some way may be felt to be the one good thing that comes out of divorce. It is something that happens almost without our realizing it and it is not limited to supporting those whose situation is similar to our own.

If we will allow it to, suffering can indeed make us gentler, warmer and more open. I have seen an apparently cold woman transformed by the suffering attendant on her husband's death. Quite clearly God was with her and his Spirit was dwelling in her in that time of pain. The result was a new person, to whom others were instinctively attracted. It is a quality that has never left her and is a source of comfort and inspiration to many.

In this sense of sharing we do not have to learn how to do it so much as to accept the particular blessing that God has given us. It may be demanding of both time and energy, but it is here that we can see how suffering can be used creatively, leading us in new directions in our lives and into new paths of service to God.

Just as there are many different forms of suffering, so it seems there are many ways in which it may be seen as a privilege. We may not understand why it happens, but that does not matter. What matters is that we can expect to meet God in our suffering and to find that he uses it and us to his glory. That, above all, is our God-given privilege.

FOR BIBLE READING AND MEDITATION
Read the story of Jesus's agony and betrayal in Mark 14, and focus particularly on verses 27–42:

'You will all fall away', Jesus told them, 'for it is written:

> "I will strike the shepherd,
> and the sheep will be scattered."

But after I have risen, I will go ahead of you into Galilee.'

Peter declared, 'Even if all fall away, I will not.'

'I tell you the truth,' Jesus answered, 'today – yes, tonight – before the cock crows twice you yourself will disown me three times.'

But Peter insisted emphatically, 'Even if I have to die with you, I will never disown you.' And all the others said the same.

They went to a place called Gethsemane, and Jesus said to his disciples, 'Sit here while I pray.' He took Peter, James and John along with him, and he began to be deeply distressed and troubled. 'My soul is overwhelmed with sorrow to the point of death,' he said to them. 'Stay here and keep watch.'

Going a little farther, he fell to the ground and prayed that if possible the hour might pass from him.

'*Abba,* Father,' he said, 'everything is possible for you. Take this cup from me. Yet not what I will, but what you will.'

Then he returned to his disciples and found them sleeping. 'Simon,' he said to Peter, 'are you asleep? Could you not keep watch for one hour? Watch and pray so that you will not fall into temptation. The spirit is willing, but the body is weak.'

Once more he went away and prayed the same thing. When he came back, he again found them sleeping, because their eyes were heavy. They did not know what to say to him.

Returning the third time, he said to them, 'Are you still sleeping and resting? Enough! The hour is come. Look, the Son of Man is betrayed into the hands of sinners. Rise! Let us go! Here comes my betrayer!'

Here we find all human weakness exemplified in the behaviour of the closest disciples of Jesus, and witness the ultimate in human suffering in Jesus's agony in Gethsemane.

First, the disciples. It was not through any lack of love for Jesus or lack of faith in him that they failed him in his greatest need. Not just Peter but all the disciples insisted that they would never 'disown' Jesus. When a charismatic leader, or simply a loved one, is physically present it is easy to proclaim utter loyalty to him or her. It is in their absence that the expression of this ideal begins to falter. The ideal crumbles away when it does not accord with physical well-being or even with popular opinion. So it was to be with Peter, while the other disciples did not even stay around long enough to risk the confrontation.

The disciples also failed Jesus in a way that we might at first find understandable and be slow to condemn. Giving in to what was no doubt extreme physical and emotional tiredness the chosen three, like the rest, fell asleep. Willingly or unwillingly they opted out of the drama which was unfolding before them. Peter, James and John who had previously witnessed the transfiguration of Jesus failed to understand that they had again been singled out to share in something special. Jesus's command, 'Watch and pray so that you will not fall into temptation', suggests a spiritual battle, from which the disciples in their human weakness drew back. It is here quite clear that a general willingness is not enough. To follow Jesus requires complete commitment in all areas of our lives, whatever our natural inclinations may be. Simply falling asleep was a devastating betrayal of the ideal.

Jesus understands, then, these sins of omission – denial of support and a reluctance to break natural routines – which most of us have experienced ourselves and inflicted on others, to a greater or lesser extent, in our lives. These acts of betrayal by the disciples represent very broadly all that human beings can do to each other in their personal relationships. Only here it is the Son of God who is on the receiving end, Jesus who understood and who on the cross prayed on behalf of us all, 'Father forgive them for they do not know what they are doing' (Luke 23.34).

Secondly, Jesus himself. The words, 'My soul is overwhelmed with sorrow to the point of death,' express the unparalleled magnitude of his suffering. Like us he longs to be spared it and his prayer must surely strike a chord in all our hearts: is it not possible for God's purpose to be worked out without all this agony? It is important, when we remember the cross, not to lose sight of the spiritual and emotional dimension to Jesus's pain, which all too often we fail to appreciate or think is peculiar to ourselves. 'The Son of Man is betrayed into the hands of sinners,' has been described as 'the most terrible [verse] in Mark', for in it God's chosen people not only reject Jesus but deliberately turn him over to the heathen nations (the 'sinners') so that they can inflict their worst torture on him.[8]

Jesus, then, not only knows far more than we ever can about suffering. He also understands how thoroughly unwelcome it is and how readily we can betray our own principles to avoid it. It is not hard to transfer all this to individual human circumstances and in particular to the breakdown or loss of relationships. When we do this, it is important to remember that there is light at the end of the tunnel. We may not understand this at the time, just as the disciples did not understand Jesus's promise: 'After I have risen I will go ahead of you into Galilee', but the promise and its fulfilment are there nonetheless.

Make one or more of the following verses your own prayer:

> The Lord himself goes before you and will be with you; he will never leave you nor forsake you. Do not be afraid; do not be discouraged.   (Deut. 31.8)

> You hear, O Lord, the desire of the afflicted; you encourage them and you listen to their cry, defending the fatherless and the oppressed, in order that man, who is of the earth, may terrify no more.   (Ps. 10.17–18)

> Let us fix our eyes on Jesus . . . who for the joy set before him endured the cross, scorning its shame, and sat down at the right hand of the throne of God. Consider him, who endured such opposition from sinful men, so that you will not grow weary and lose heart.   (Heb. 12.2–3)

> And I heard a loud voice from the throne saying, 'Now the dwelling of God is with men, and he will live with them. They will be his people, and God himself will be with them and be their God. He will wipe every tear from their eyes. There will be no more death or mourning or crying or pain, for the old order of things has passed away'.   (Rev. 21.3–4)

May the God of hope fill you with all joy and peace as you trust in him, so that you may overflow with hope by the power of the Holy Spirit.   (Rom. 15.13)

Suggestions for further reading
Charles Ohlrich's *The Suffering God* (Triangle, 1983) is excellent. Equally good, but slightly more complex, is Paul Tournier's *Creative Suffering* (SCM Press, 1982). Both books refer to further works on the subject.

References
1 Quoted in B. Sibley, *Shadowlands* (Hodder 1985), p.151.
2 C. Ohlrich, *The Suffering God* (Triangle 1983), p.102.
3 ibid.
4 Swihart and Brigham, op.cit., p.11.
5 Küng, op.cit., p.579.
6 C.S. Lewis, *The Four Loves* (1960, reprinted Fount 1977), p.112.
7 Küng, op.cit., pp.578–9.
8 R.H. Lightfoot, quoted by D.E. Nineham, in *Saint Mark* (Penguin 1963), p.393.

3

A Place in the Family

In the first two chapters we were looking quite deliberately inwards at the emotions and suffering that emerge from marriage breakdown. I have tried to show what it feels like when a marriage ends and what sort of outside help is most appropriate. I have done this because I know only too well that you cannot get on with the business of living the rest of your life, let alone using that life in some positive way, until you have taken an objective and constructive look at what is going on inside you. When you are able to say 'Yes, I am lonely,' or 'Yes, I do feel miserable and inadequate and please, God, help,' only then is it really possible to stop looking inwards and turn your attention to what lies outside and ahead.

This chapter is a transitional one. We shall be moving on from the inner feelings of an individual to his or her immediate surroundings. This is because I feel sure that many divorced people need to learn to function once again as a family unit in order to find the confidence and security to face the world at large on equal terms once again. I use the word 'family' in its widest sense, for it is a transition which is as necessary for someone left alone to make as for someone left with children.

Structures

When I was a student I lived for a while with a chemist. Part of her basic equipment was a set of coloured balls which she would fit together on plastic stalks to represent molecular structures. It always looked much more fun than the essays and translations assigned to us language students! This toy of hers could in fact be used to illustrate a basic structural principle: remove one ball on its stalk and you are left not with an incomplete structure but with a new one, whose elements are in a slightly different relationship to one another. The same is true if a new ball and stalk are added – both the structure and the relationships within it are changed.

Just as molecules build up chemical structures, so people form social ones. If a person leaves or joins a group, be it a household, family, church or club, that social structure will change, however imperceptibly.

The point I want to make is that families are like that. If one family member leaves the home, the structure re-forms without him or her into a new one. It is normal human behaviour to close the gap and not to leave the place at table unfilled or the bedroom untouched. When people do behave in this way it is usually looked on as an unhealthy form of grief or mourning.

Changed, not Broken

Now I am convinced that one of the cruellest labels our twentieth century society has coined, most often with respect to children, is that of the 'broken' home. Broken marriages need not, and should not, automatically entail all that has been implied by that label. It is, moreover, unspeakably painful for a lone parent to hear his or her child referred to as coming from a broken home. There are over-tones of delinquency, domestic violence, social deprivation and so on. Happily, the current tendency is to use the more neutral terms 'one-parent' or 'single-parent' family, cover-ing all parents on their own, whatever the reason for it. This has the advantage of dissociating the family unit from a whole range of social problems with which it might have been associated, if only by implication.

A home is no less a home because one of its founder members has left it, whether voluntarily (as in separation) or involuntarily (through death). But to people who are acutely aware of the absence of a loved one this is far from obvious. Even Christians who know in their minds that God is no less present in their midst than he was before, may still have difficulty in believing it in their hearts.

All this applies with equal force to the wider Christian family. The loss of one member means not only a change in the make up of the whole church family, but also a change in the relationship of that group of Christians to the family that has suffered the loss.

Fortunately, people are more than plastic representations of molecules. People are not simply draughts on a board to be moved around and taken away without further thought. It is easy enough to talk about restructuring family units, but it is one of the hardest things in the world to do, not least because it is bound up with some or all of the emotions I have already described. Nonetheless, I believe it is an essential early step for Christians to regain confidence in their own family setting and to feel reassured of their place in the church family. Once this happens the way is wide open to them to consider future directions, knowing that any changes in lifestyle rest on a firm and secure basis of family relationships.

A Changed Family Unit

The concepts of home and family, at least as we commonly understand them, do not figure greatly in the pages of the New Testament. God, in his infinite wisdom, does not set before us a model of Mum and Dad and 1.8 children (or whatever the current rate may be). The average home in New Testament times probably housed a much more extensive family unit than is usual nowadays, at least in Western

Europe, but we are also given glimpses of other patterns, such as the household of Mary and Martha and their brother Lazarus.

Very much more important for the New Testament writers is the concept of relationships, the supreme model being that of Jesus to his Father. It is a relationship that is expressed in Greek by words that mean 'being in' or 'dwelling in', and the marvellous thing is that it is a relationship which we can share in too. If you look carefully at John 17.20–26, you will see that Jesus's prayer, which is so often quoted in the context of church unity, is first and foremost a prayer for individuals – for you and me – to enter this special relationship of 'oneness', ' . . . that the love you have for me may be in them and that I myself may be in them' (17.26). What is more, it is a relationship that Jesus promises to anyone who loves him: 'My Father will love him, and we will come to him and make our home with him' (John 14.23).

Now surely for Christians, who have the privilege of such a special relationship, it is this that must be at the centre of our lives. If we hold on to this promise – which perhaps has already been realized in our lives – then we have nothing to fear when human relationships let us down.

Well, you may say, that's all very fine, but how does it help anyone to cope practically with having to be both father and mother to their children, or managing alone a home that was meant for a couple? I think that at least part of the answer is that God draws us together with him into a new family unit, whether it is one person, or two or three or more. This, certainly, has been my experience, and I associate the beginning of being able to 'cope' with one particular event – a service which included the laying on of hands.

This came at the end of a week's holiday, our first, at Lee Abbey. In the course of the final Eucharist many of us went forward for prayer. When it came to my turn and hands were laid upon me, the prayer was a very simple one, committing me and my children into God's hands; I added my own silent prayer, asking God to come into my life. The effect was instantaneous: I felt a great load being lifted from me and was overwhelmed with joy and peace. Now this sort of experience is one familiar to countless numbers of Christians in all kinds of circumstances, but for me one of its most significant aspects was the intense love that I then felt for my children. Not that I did not love them before – I did. But that love was somehow transformed as we were all brought into oneness with God and with each other. It no longer mattered if the world looked at us and imagined brokenness, for it was clear to me that we had found wholeness in God.

It is God's peace that brings about wholeness in a home, regardless of the number of people who live there and the pattern of their relationship t each other. And this peace and wholeness communicates itself to others. This does not, of course, mean that there are not times when we may long for a missing partner or feel a deep sense of loss (particularly when a pipe bursts or the dinner burns!). But such moments will not harm the new structure unless we consciously allow it to happen, and turn our backs on God in our midst.

This is equally true in bereavement. I have a friend who is a widow and who greatly misses her much-loved husband. It would have been easy for her to retreat into her grief and allow her home to become no more than a half-empty house. Instead, her nearness to God has ensured that her home remains just that, a home filled with God's peace. Such a peace stems from my friend's knowledge of God and her acceptance of her situation while, in her heart, she longs for the life to come.

So it is for a divorced Christian or, indeed, for someone who has never married. God takes the unit that exists, just as it is, and makes it the object of his gifts.

However, unlike bereavement or singleness, divorce can involve the family unit in other, more complex, relationships. If a former partner remarries, perhaps has children, then the husband, wife or children left behind are drawn into situations with a new set of problems. Does it really make sense to claim 'wholeness' for a home where the children disappear with the absent parent for weekends or holidays, or where there is a real danger of jealousy or bitterness? The answer is yes, it does make sense. God will strengthen the new family unit so that it does not need to be totally exclusive, any more than good marriages need a protective wall built round them. However hard it may seem at first, confidence in the new structure enables its members to withstand any threats, real or apparent, and to be healthily open to other relationships as well. The writer of Proverbs knew this, whether or not he had a precise situation in mind: 'Trust in the Lord with all your heart and lean not on your own understanding; in all your ways acknowledge him and he will make your paths straight' (Prov. 3.5–6).

A Changed Place in the Christian Family

We do not need the help of structural diagrams to know that any change within the family automatically brings about some degree of change in relationships between that family and those outside it. For example, most people who have been bereaved or divorced can testify to a sudden drop in certain kinds of social invitations. It is easy to recognize, within the security of marriage, that some invitations only come our way because we are one of a couple, but this does not make it any easier to accept when they stop coming afterwards.

This may seem like rejection, but it is not necessarily so. One problem is sheer embarrassment. As we have already seen, people find it hard to cope with their friends' marriages breaking up, Christians in particular. They may long to invite a friend in this position to their homes and lack the courage to do so. Consequently he or she feels too hurt to say anything and a damaging vicious circle results.

The greatest difficulty for outsiders tends to be knowing what to say. There is not just the communication problem referred to already in chapter 1, where the person suffering has trouble communicating that pain: it works the other way round as well. Yet neither the divorced nor the bereaved want to be left alone to 'get over it' until such time as other people feel comfortable with them again. As I have suggested it is quite possible for visitors to follow a simple list of do's and don't's, perhaps in consultation with a pastor or with someone who has gone through the same experience. For example, just as it is unhelpful for the bereaved to be regaled with stories of other people's illnesses and misfortunes, so it is equally unhelpful for an abandoned wife or husband to have to hear their visitor's opinion of the other partner. 'I always knew he/she was no good for you' is an extraordinarily hurtful comment; after all, the couple loved each other once and maybe still do. Similarly to say how marvellous the other person was is only to add tacit disapproval to the weight of guilt already felt. Other members of the church family, therefore, will need to recognize that there is inevitably awkwardness on both sides and that they need to choose words carefully. This is even more true when it comes to prayer. To pray for God's help and guidance is one thing; to ask that he will bring back/prosper/ pour out his wrath upon the absent partner is quite another!

A further problem is that other people often recognize and accept the change from being a couple to being single much more rapidly than the person concerned is able to come to terms with that change. The tendency is to class people as 'alone' before they are ready for it, and the Christian community is no exception in this.

It is a hard lesson for people to learn that they have in the past often been seen in terms of a marriage or family unit rather than as individuals, but it does show the value of making new relationships on the basis of being one instead of trying to keep to those previously made on the basis of being two. This is not, of course, to suggest that all old friends will drop away, merely that the friendship will probably take a different direction. Conversely, new relationships based on the new family unit will certainly evolve spontaneously and naturally, however unlikely it may seem at times.

It is no good saying that within the Christian family it ought perhaps to be different. Certainly we are right to expect a deeper level of love and compassion from our brothers and sisters in Christ. But this will manifest itself in a variety of new ways, and it is unrealistic – and ultimately unproductive – to expect nothing to be changed. Considerable demands may be made on both sides. For example, a family that was previously self-sufficient may now, in a moment of crisis, need to be taken lock, stock and barrel (or children, rabbits and guinea pigs) into someone else's home for the duration. Are other families in the community ready to take them in? Is the family in trouble prepared to accept their help? When they are, then we see some deeply committed friendships emerging.

Difficulties like these are encountered by Christians and non-Christians alike. For Christians, though, there is an added complication, namely the importance which the Church now attaches to the idea of the family. If anything could be guaranteed to reinforce the feeling of failure when a marriage ends and the family is depleted, it is surely this!

Part of the problem, perhaps, is the use of the image of the Church as God's family. The trouble is that it is such a good image. The love which we singularly fail to extend to our neighbour in the pew should indeed be a family love, with the total acceptance of one another and the commitment that such love implies. What better way of describing the body of Christ than in terms of an earthly family – an idea which we can easily grasp. But inevitably the comparison gets used the other way round: if the Church is a 'family', then our Christian duty is to improve our own family life at home, to make it worthy of the image that we ourselves, following biblical tradition, have emphasized so much. Again, there is nothing essentially wrong in this, but we do need to be careful that some element of intolerance does not creep in here. There is a danger that those who live alone or those whose family life does not accord with this Christian 'norm' may feel themselves to be left out, or regarded in some way as less 'Christian' than others.

It is quite natural that however caring and supportive the church to which we belong may be, most of us at times give in to our self-pity and feel rejected. When this happens I believe that we must ask ourselves in all honesty whether we have lost sight of the real reason for the family image, which is to express our relationship with God as well as to each other: 'We are God's children . . . heirs of God and co-heirs with Christ, if indeed we share in his sufferings in order that we may also share in his glory' (Rom. 8.16–17). We are God's children – each one of us – and the Church is God's people; not the buildings, not the administration, not the governmental structures, but the *people* are God's people. David Watson, in his book *I Believe in the Church,* says that this is 'the most thrilling "good news" that [many] could ever hear'[1] and he quotes 1 John 3.1: 'How great is the love the Father has lavished on us, that we should be called children of God! And that is what we are!' No need, then, to feel rejected, for we are already part of that wider community called by God to share his blessings, an extension of the Old Testament covenant community (and goodness knows, they got themselves into enough trouble over the years!).

Where does the divorced Christian fit into the church community? We must recognize from the outset that this community is full of human imperfections. If we fail to see this we shall hurt others and very quickly get hurt ourselves, and of course if it were a perfect community we could not hope to be part of it anyway. The answer I think depends on the relationships that we make within this Christian family.

The biggest hurdle to get over is the lack of confidence, that feeling of inadequacy, that we looked at in chapter 1. All Christians, but most particularly those who seem not to conform to the standard pattern, must believe that they have something to offer. If you are not in church one Sunday morning, then the rest of the congregation is the poorer for it and is affected by it. Everyone has his or her place in the community and everyone matters, both to God and to the other members of his family.

It is tempting to feel that relationships with other Christians are bound to be one-sided, particularly if much has already been received from them in the way of love and support in prayer and practical help. This is never true! As we saw in chapter 2, experience of suffering leads to sharing the lessons of that with others, and we shall be looking again (in chapter 6) at some particular forms of service that divorced Christians may want to offer the church itself. Suffice it to say for the moment that an increased awareness of God's love and forgiveness and of having met God in suffering is more than enough to ensure new and fruitful relationships, and a very positive contribution to the corporate life of the church.

In practical terms this means that local church leaders should be encouraged to treat the family of a divorced Christian in the same way as any other. Where it is appropriate, then, the family (which also means an individual on his or her own) might take their turn at hosting meetings and supper parties, putting up overnight visitors, and so on. In this way the feeling of not being different, of wholeness, will receive welcome reinforcement from the wider church family.

It also means, of course, that a much larger group of people than just casual visitors will be called upon to show love and understanding to the family in question. Sunday School teachers, for example, will need to take care not to make a child feel awkward because he spends some Sundays away with the other parent; church members will need to learn to accept the absence of children without question and not appear too inquisitive about their welfare.

It is worth bearing in mind that the dividing line between loving concern and idle curiosity is a very thin one and, as I have already said, it is almost inevitable that people will be hurt by something or other. When this happens there needs to be complete honesty between all concerned. Perhaps a mutual friend will have to explain to X how a remark has been misinterpreted by Y as criticism or scandal-mongering, while Y is cautioned about over-sensitivity and self-consciousness.

In this chapter I have tried to stress two things. The first is that when divorce happens the family is obviously different, but that wholeness can nonetheless be restored. Secondly, that family and its individual members now also have a slightly changed place in the Christian family. But, and it is a big but, they do have a place and they are there to play their part in that family, both giving and receiving, alongside everyone else.

Given that the Church is a fallible human institution, it would be wrong to pretend that all is then sweetness and light. There will always be those who find divorced Christians hard to accept and who will not necessarily hide their feelings. However hard it may seem, it is important to realize that such feelings are not usually irrational or based on personal prejudice, but spring from a deep conviction of the indissolubility of marriage. Even if this belief produces uncharitable behaviour on the part of those holding it, such a conviction commands respect. But, similarly, those who feel this should remember too that it is not easy for a Christian who is assured of God's love and forgiveness to be denied that forgiveness by God's people.

In the end it is a test of love. Can I love someone who condemns my past behaviour and present situation? Can you love someone who has acted in defiance of a principle you hold dear? In 1983, Church of England Diocesan Synods were asked to debate 'Option G', which offered a possible way forward for the remarriage of divorced people in church. At one local meeting a leading churchman spoke vehemently against the 'scum' in his parish, whose children played in the street and went off with Dad and his woman on Saturdays; he urged Synod to reject any idea of sanctioning remarriage on the grounds of increased social depravity. It was an amazing speech which ignored the fact that the marriages of Christians and other 'decent' people also break down, took no account of Synod members who were themselves divorced, and displayed a quite remarkable lack of love. Yet there was no doubt that his words came from the heart. If the Church as a whole were to present such a stance to the world, what hope would we ever have of proclaiming Christ's gospel of love and repentance?

Jesus asked: 'If you love those who love you, what reward will you get? . . . And if you greet only your brothers, what are you doing more than others?' (Matt.5.46–47), and he concluded with the command 'Be perfect . . . as your heavenly Father is perfect' (Matt. 5.48). Once we make love our aim, in the light of God's love for us, our place in the Christian family and God's place in our hearts and homes are both beyond all doubt.

FOR BIBLE READING AND PRAYER
Read 1 John 4.7–21:

Dear friends, let us love one another, for love comes from God. Everyone who loves has been born of God and knows God. Whoever does not love does not know God, because God is love.
This is how God showed his love among us: He sent his one

and only Son into the world that we might live through him. This is love: not that we loved God, but that he loved us and sent his Son as an atoning sacrifice for our sins. Dear friends, since God so loved us, we also ought to love one another. No one has ever seen God; but if we love one another, God lives in us and his love is made complete in us.

We know that we live in him and he in us, because he has given us of his Spirit. And we have seen and testify that the Father has sent his Son to be the Saviour of the world. If anyone acknowledges that Jesus is the Son of God, God lives in him and he in God. And so we know and rely on the love God has for us.

God is love. Whoever lives in love lives in God, and God in him. Love is made complete among us so that we will have confidence on the day of judgment, because in this world we are like him. There is no fear in love. But perfect love drives out fear, because fear has to do with punishment. The man who fears is not made perfect in love.

We love because he first loved us. If anyone says, 'I love God,' yet hates his brother, he is a liar. For anyone who does not love his brother, whom he has seen, cannot love God, whom he has not seen. And he has given us this command. Whoever loves God must also love his brother.

We have already seen (from John 17.25–6) the ideal relationship between Jesus and his Father, a relationship which is offered to all Christians to enjoy. In this passage from the first letter of John, the writer shows us that our relationship of love with God *is* our love for one another.

How would you define love? Here it is defined quite simply as God's love, a love which gives everything for those who are loved, however little they deserve it. Our response to this is inevitably a pathetic reflection of God's love for us, but we can see how loving God is indissolubly linked to loving one another. Notice too the close association between love and life. To love is to live. We may know this in some measure from our own relationships, in marriage or friendship. But loving God does more for us than just making us feel good: it is life-giving. 'Whoever lives in love lives in God and God in him' is a great promise for us here and now.

In this passage we are offered reassurance about love. Unlike so many human relationships there is no fear involved: no fear of losing the loved one, no fear of our own inadequacy. We can confidently put aside failed or imperfect relationships in the light of God's promise.

We are twice reminded, at the beginning and end of this passage, that God's promise of love is for all of us. It is not restricted to the people we ourselves happen to like and love; the people who are critical of us and those with whom we feel we have nothing in common also know and love God and are loved by him. We must recognize this and learn to set aside hurt, antipathy, indifference, in order to love them too. Only then can we begin to understand something of God's love for us. So, then, knowing that we are filled with God's love, we are to go out and show *our* love to all those with whom we are in contact, and to rejoice in the love of other Christians for us, that God's love may be 'made complete in us'.

Now read Colossians 3.12–17 to see what our love for one another means in practice.

> Heavenly Father, thank you for your perfect love for us. Forgive us for the times we ignore your love and for the times we substitute human love as an ideal instead. Help us to love one another better, that we may grow closer to one another and to you, according to your will. And may your love and peace rule in our hearts. Amen.

Suggestions for further reading
Chapter 6 of David Watson's *I Believe in the Church* (Hodder & Stoughton 1978) is entitled 'The People of God' and

covers some of the points raised in this chapter. Joyce Huggett, *Conflict: Friend or Foe?* (Kingsway 1984) is readable and relevant, as is Margaret Britton, *The Single Woman in the Family of God* (Epworth Press 1982) a book which admits to a slight feminist bias.

References
1   D. Watson, *I Believe in the Church* (Hodder & Stoughton 1978), p.76.

PART II

Looking Outwards

Introduction to Part II

We have seen in Part I how marriage breakdown demands a certain amount of self-appraisal and reassessment. I have suggested that this might be done both by looking inward and working through all the emotions bound up with separation, and also by looking at one's immediate environment and the inevitable changes there. In this second section we shall be moving away from 'inner' problems and feelings in order to consider some of the new directions that life can take after divorce or separation.

Like any other significant event in life – leaving home, moving house, getting married, having children and so on – divorce brings with it several possible changes in direction. It should not be taken as implying any kind of moral judgement if divorce is viewed as the basis for a fresh start. Just as any form of suffering can be used constructively, so divorce can be regarded in a more positive light by looking forward to new opportunities rather than in a negative one by harping back on failure. There are many Christians whose lives bear testimony to this, although it is something that is easily overlooked. It is inevitable in any community that people are more immediately aware of the needs of those who have not coped, or who have been unable to come to terms with their situation, than of those who have bounced back.

This does not mean to say either that divorce is something to be proud of. There are plenty of trendy people around who are happy to attribute their success to getting divorced, describing it as the best thing they ever did. For the Christian this can never be the honest truth. But the knowledge that God has wiped the slate clean is a good reason for planning a somewhat different life in the future, and this can also be of very real psychological benefit. An excellent model is the description of the call of Isaiah, where forgiveness is immediately followed by the offer of a new direction. In his vision the prophet is approached by a seraph holding a live coal from the altar:

> With it he touched my mouth and said, 'See, this has touched your lips; your guilt is taken away and your sin atoned for.' Then I heard the voice of the Lord saying, 'Whom shall I send? And who will go for us?' And I said, 'Here I am. Send me!' (Isa. 6.7–8).

In the last section I tried to show how divorce inevitably means difference, and how this difference has to be acknowledged rather than concealed if genuine relationships are to be established or maintained. In the same way that difference has to underlie the pattern of life in the future. New patterns of work, of home life and of church life all need to be worked out on the basis of the new 'family' unit. The fact of being divorced need not be proclaimed from the rooftops, but neither should it be totally ignored. The remaining chapters attempt to explore some new ways ahead on that basis.

4

New Directions at Home

In the last chapter I touched on the question of the home and suggested that a home is not 'broken' by the absence of one of its original members. This is a theme which I should like to develop a little further as we come to consider some of the ways in which the home can offer a new direction to the life of a divorced Christian.

A Christian home is not defined according to the number of people who live in it or their relationship to one another. To call a home Christian is to say something about the nature of the relationship between the people who live there – if indeed there is more than one person – and about their relationship to others, as well as to God. It implies a welcome and a concern for visitors, and even for strangers; it is a place where life is lived as closely as possible in accordance with the life and love of Christ, and it is probably the place where this is found hardest to do.

The home seems to be the obvious place to start, because it is here that the greatest change has taken place and the most adjustments have to be made. The home is also somewhere of great opportunity, where the world may expect to find bitterness and instead see love; where peace and wholeness may be found instead of disharmony and bitterness; in short where the world may sense the presence of God. As David Prior writes: 'A Christian home is not simply a family which goes to church on Sundays: it is a home where Christ is real, day in, day out', and his conclusion is that 'there is . . . no more powerful evangelistic weapon than a Christian home where the love of God motivates every relationship'.[1] To create such a home is the task of all Christians, whatever their circumstances. If you are divorced, how can you best meet its challenge?

Problems

Let's begin by admitting that there are problems, which are both practical and emotional – we have not left them all behind in Part I! Confronting them and dealing with them is a necessary preliminary if the home is in any way to resemble the definition just quoted.

At the end of a marriage there are, inevitably, major practical problems that are firmly rooted in the home. Many people will find themselves having to cope single-handed with situations previously handled only by their partner (e.g. child care, property maintenance), or having to make do with fewer possessions and less money with which to replace things that were jointly owned. In short, the practical arrangements of everyday life, which are manageable enough when shared, can be formidable and daunting when the other person drops out.

There is no simple solution to this. However, one very good source of help and advice (beyond the 'official' agencies of solicitors, builders and so on) is to be found in single friends or relations. People who are used to living alone are well qualified to help others cope with everyday practical problems. They can show you how much you can reasonably expect to handle on your own, when outside help is needed, and where to get it from. Seek out the single people in your own church and ask their advice; they will feel valued because of it and will be pleased to help.

Anyone who has both a job outside the home and children to look after can testify to the problem of housework. When you are separated this may be the last straw, and possibly a sign that it is time to consider paid help in the home, even if it is no more than someone coming in to clean once a week. For myself, this is a step I have long resisted, partly out of pride – for surely I ought to be able to do my own cleaning – and partly for financial reasons: wouldn't the money be better spent on something else? Slowly I am coming round to the idea that it would not, and that if necessary something else must go. After all, God has continued to provide my family with a home and if it is not reasonably clean and tidy it will be neither good for us nor a gift that can be used in his service.

Home maintenance presents a similar problem, but it is worth remembering that some people actually enjoy painting and decorating, and it is surprising how quickly and pleasantly jobs like this can be done when friends decide to do them together. Women, no doubt, find such matters more daunting than men and may be reluctant to expose their ignorance or clumsiness to professional decorators and builders, quite apart from a fear of being taken advantage of financially. On the other hand a single father may feel equally intimidated when he has to take his child to a clinic or playgroup. The process of learning to seek help and building up confidence in one's own ability to handle such situations may often be quite a long one.

There are also emotional problems bound up with all this. To start with, the house or flat may have been the subject of legal negotiations, and it can then all too easily come to symbolize the agony of divorce. What ought to be a symbol of permanence and security can, at least for a while, stand for the exact opposite. In many respects it may be easier to move house and start again; some people will in any case find that they have to do just this, while for others it will be impossible.

The home may also become the focus for the feelings of difference and inadequacy mentioned in chapter 1. Such feelings can, sadly, be aggravated by other people's curiosity. It seems to be a fact of human nature that all the time we conform to the norm, people do not pay us much attention; but once we appear to be different, every aspect of our lives comes under scrutiny, and our household management and domestic routine tend to bear the brunt of it.

In view of all this, I think it may be true that people need time to rebuild their confidence and trust in their own home after the upset of divorce, just as they need to regain confidence in themselves and other people.

It is quite natural for any major crisis or tragedy to create a hiatus in the normal pattern of family life. For a while people are not expected to issue social invitations or to take on special responsibilities. Such a break is of course necessary, but it does have the unfortunate consequence that one day the person who has suffered the crisis has quite deliberately to restart the process of offering hospitality and generally taking the initiative in social contacts. This can be a very hard thing to do. For example, while a house-warming party is natural enough if separation has involved moving, it is quite a different kettle of fish to give a first party in the same house but without the partner whom people are used to seeing in those surroundings.

Nevertheless, opening the 'new' home and family unit to others is a very necessary stage in the process of healing and restoration. It is important to remember that although entertaining may seem to be a practical process, the main hurdle is more likely to be an emotional one. Yet it is a hurdle that has to be cleared in the course of progressing from brokenness to wholeness.

The opening verses of Isaiah 54 compare the humiliation of the defeated nation to that of a woman who is either childless or, for various reasons, without a husband. God's promise to Israel is also an expression of his love for those men and women in this analogous position. It is a promise of change that relates to the home as well as to the individual and it is a source of new hope and confidence for us:

Jerusalem, you have been like a childless woman, but now you can sing and shout for joy. Now you will have more children than a woman whose husband never left her! Make the tent you live in larger; lengthen its ropes and strengthen the pegs! You will extend your boundaries on all sides . . . Do not be afraid – you will not be disgraced again; you will not be humiliated. You will forget your unfaithfulness as a young wife, and your desperate loneliness as a widow. Your Creator will be like a husband to you – the Lord Almighty is his name. The holy God of Israel will save you – he is the ruler of all the world.   (Isa. 54.1–5, GNB)

A Home Alone?

With the practical and emotional obstacles acknowledged and confidence in the home restored, what then? A change in direction based on the home can take several forms: there may be further, deliberate, changes in the people making up that home, or changes in the specific uses to which the home is put, or a combination of both.

Now obviously I am not about to suggest that the next step after divorce is to find other people to come and live in your home, or for you to go off and join some sort of community. The question that needs to be put is what has been learned from marriage, and how can this be set to good use in the future?

It seems to me that the result of living with a partner in marriage, and perhaps also with children, is that people have learned to share; not just to share their possessions, but experiences, hopes, fears and emotions of all kinds. For the most part things are not 'mine' or 'yours', they are 'ours'. Consequently there is a certain openness to possessions that does not come so easily to many people who have always lived alone. In normal family life there is no room for temper tantrums or even irritability if someone uses 'your' stereo or eats the last of the biscuits.

Similarly there is the habit of sharing everything else: going places and doing things with another person, sharing their preoccupations. Now when that person disappears life cannot help but be empty. Yet rather than give in to loneliness it is surely desirable to exploit that inclination to share which, although it may be hard to pin down and define, is readily sensed by visitors and more than anything helps to create an atmosphere of peace and wholeness in a home.

The home of a person who has this 'inclination to share' is a relaxed place and there is an openness about it that will make it immensely attractive to other people. No matter how untidy or chaotic the house may be, the lack of tension on the part of the family as to who does what, where and how, and a willingness to accept other people as they are, which develops naturally in the course of marriage – all this makes for a real home which other people will be drawn to. It is immaterial that there may be only one person living there if that person has been used to being one of several (perhaps has never married but has come from a large family). He or she may, however, need to be reassured as to what other people like about that home and to be encouraged to use it in God's service. We shall be considering a few specific uses of the home a little later, but it is a useful first step to draw attention to this very obvious factor of atmosphere which can be built on for there to be a positive contribution both to the Christian community and to those outside it.

It may be that some people who are naturally gregarious react to marriage breakdown by deciding to open their doors to all comers – to escape from unhappiness with one person by seeking happiness with several or even with many. Certainly community living may appear an attractive alternative to one's own company, and a period spent living in such a community (away from home) could well be beneficial to some people after the end of a marriage. But it is quite another matter to start one yourself, and something that demands much courage, prayer and, probably, support from your own church. A number of books have been written about experiments in extended households or community living, and the best of them stress the problems as much as the rewards. It is not something to be embarked upon lightly, nor on your own, as will be suggested again below.

One further word of warning. Much of what is said in this chapter must be modified, perhaps even ignored, if there are children in the home. John Woolmer, in writing about extended households warns that 'constant open doors are unsettling for children' and reminds Christian parents that the first call on their ministry comes from within the home itself.[2] How much more true is this likely to be for children who have already been unsettled by their parents' separation. Yet single parents will also want their children to be aware of the continuing love of other Christian friends, so each family will need to work out its own solution to the question of privacy.

Challenges at Home

Hospitality

Three things about hospitality, the most obvious way to use a home. Firstly, hospitality is required of all of us who have the privilege of a roof over our heads, whether the accommodation is functional or palatial. Peter tells the early Church to 'offer hospitality to one another without grumbling' (1 Pet. 4.9), and the Epistle to Titus puts being hospitable at the top of the list of qualities required of an overseer or bishop (Titus 1.8). Secondly, although it is something we all do in some way, hospitality, like evangelism, is a gift. Those who excel at it need to have that recognized and be encouraged in it, as with any other gift from God. But this does not absolve the rest of us from doing our share, any more than the existence of professional evangelists lets us off having to talk about our faith.

Thirdly, we are not, collectively speaking, particularly good at offering hospitality. Perhaps it is the British reserve again, but we are reluctant to let visitors share to the full our homes and possessions in the way that those from other cultures often expect us to. It is perhaps reassuring to discover the phrase 'without grumbling' in 1 Peter 4.9 and to deduce that the first Christians were not always as hospitable as they might have been, despite their different social structure.

Most people will have their own advice to offer on the subject of hospitality. Mine is twofold: first, be natural, and second, know your limits and keep within them. This means, for instance, not undertaking a formal dinner party for a dozen if you panic at the thought of feeding more than six, or if such an occasion is just not your 'scene'. We do not have to step outside our own limits to make the love of God known effectively. We can get on with the job of showing that love to people we naturally come into contact with, and leave the rest to someone else. John Perry talks of a young mother on a housing estate who 'opened her home for mothers and toddlers and in many other practical ways unconsciously conveyed the love of Jesus'.[3] This person was offering hospitality to those she was alongside and in a form appropriate to her situation, to great effect.

There are divorced people all around us if we choose to open our eyes to the fact, and to offer hospitality to friends and acquaintances in that situation is to bear direct witness to the love of God for them and us. Children are a marvellous point of contact in this respect, as parents whose paths would normally never cross get to know each other at the school gate and elsewhere.

Hospitality need not, of course, have a 'hidden agenda' of evangelism. If we come back to the idea of being used to sharing the home with others, this might lead, for example, to offering to put up short-term visitors to the Christian community. This sort of entertaining is a valuable contribution to the community and such visits may in turn be found to have their own good effects. Those who have been bereaved, for instance, may benefit enormously from having to make an effort to look after someone again for a limited period. Since hospitality almost always involves receiving as well as giving, we should perhaps be rather more ready than we are to ask people to give their homes in service in this way.

The Home as a Meeting Place

Using your home as a place for people to meet often springs initially out of necessity. If you are a single parent with young children you will know all about the difficulties of getting out in the evenings or at weekends. But although having a Christian meeting or activity move to your home may start off as a solution to the babysitter problem, this can also be the beginning of a very real ministry to others. At first you may be just acting as host to a group already in existence, but this can already be a valuable service. A group, whether it meets to pray, study, make music or do something quite different, will be sensitive to its surroundings. A home characterized by peace and wholeness will quite unobtrusively communicate these qualities to those who meet there regularly. Not only will the life of the group benefit, but the individual members are likely to feel drawn back again, if not to the group then to the home as a place they associate with Christian love.

There are, of course, all kinds of groups that need a meeting place and they do not have to be specifically Christian to benefit from meeting in a Christian home. Some people will want to think about hosting or even initiating such a group which reflects their personal interests, whether these are political, cultural, self-help schemes or whatever.

Similarly within the Christian community individuals might consider using their homes to pursue particular activities. If you have contacts with missionaries overseas, for instance, you may decide to use your living room for playing a tape or showing a film about them, or using your garden for a fund-raising coffee morning. Look for a gap in an area of Christian life to which you yourself feel drawn, and see whether the use of your own home can help fill it. Virtually any interest which is pursued by people in their homes can be taken up by a group meeting in the same place – music, handicraft, children's activities, study and learning, to name but a few.

There is one form of Christian service in the home that deserves special mention, and that is the formation of a house group. Obviously this is not done without full consultation with the local church and needs the involvement of someone with the right gifts of leadership if you do not possess them yourself. But the importance of such groups and, not least, of the homes in which they meet, cannot be stressed enough. John Perry describes them as an essential part of church life in many places and 'a springboard for effective evangelism and social action in their neighbourhoods'. He adds: 'In the informality, group members have found the help they have needed for spiritual growth coupled with a deeper quality of fellowship.' [4] It is hard to think of a better use to which a home may be put, and with meetings happening either in the evenings or during the school day this can be wholly compatible with the needs of young children.

If none of these ideas seem appropriate, it is worth casting an eye round the home and seeing just what could be of use to other people. A long, uncluttered floor space, for example, could be a boon to a banner-making group looking for somewhere to work, and, incidentally, the source of new friendships. Or look at the furniture: a piano for a music student looking for somewhere to practise? Or a piece of technical equipment (tools, home computer) that could be shared regularly with someone, perhaps on a cost-sharing basis? With a bit of imagination you can find all sorts of uses for your home as a place for groups of individuals, and in so doing share something of God's love with them.

Home-based Evangelism

In Acts 18 we read about a character called Apollos. He spoke in the synagogue 'with great fervour' but did not know the whole truth about Jesus. So, we learn, Priscilla and Aquila took him home and 'explained to him the way of God more adequately' (Acts 18.26). They used their home, therefore, not only to talk about Jesus, but in so doing to build up the ministry of this gifted man. As a result Apollos's teaching gifts were used by the disciples for the benefit of newcomers and in public debate.

And so it is today. The place where evangelism is done most, and done effectively, is not in the church building or even in a tent where an evangelist has led hundreds to Christ: the hard work of conversion and follow-up is done at home. It may be in the homes of the people seeking Christ or in the homes of those who help them, or both. The crucial thing is that people are met in a place where they can be relaxed and receptive, a place where they can come without fear of being attacked or 'got at'.

Now you do not have to have obvious evangelistic gifts to offer your home in this way, although the chances are that you will have your own role to play. If your church is involved in a mission you might be asked to host an evangelistic supper party. However, this involves rather more than just having a large room where a couple of dozen people can eat and talk comfortably. It means being ready to invite your non-Christian friends to an occasion which will include Christians talking about what they believe. This, arguably, takes more courage than doing the actual talk (I speak from experience, having done both). But having done it once, you will become conscious of many, perhaps more modest, ways in which you and your home can be used for evangelism among your friends. This goes on all the time, in small groups, very informally and over a long period, wherever the church is strong.

David Watson uses the example of the story of the woman of Samaria (John 4) to make the point that evangelism can be done anywhere. He says: 'Some of the best opportunities for evangelism occur quite naturally in ordinary, everyday settings: in a bus-queue, a railway compartment, a hospital ward – anywhere!'[5] Now if we pause to work out how much time we spend in our homes compared with other places and think about the people who come there, the home is an obvious place to think of as having an important role in our evangelism.

Perhaps even more significant is the fact that our homes are where our personal lifestyle is exposed for what it is, particularly, of course, if there are children about to reveal anything we might wish to conceal! In a more recent book David Watson declares that the lifestyle of most Western Christians and churches is 'scarcely distinguishable' from the affluent society all around.[6] This is probably true, but in families where there is a genuine desire to spend enough but no more on themselves – to make do with black and white TV instead of colour, to buy bicycles rather than cars – it is only really in their homes that these details and the reason for them becomes apparent. Similarly, as we have already seen, it is in the home that our inclination to share our possessions may be seen for what it is. When non-Christian friends and neighbours sense in addition to an atmosphere of happiness and peace a desire to share and not to seek more than we need, this speaks volumes for the message about Jesus that we may proclaim with our lips.

Finally, the home is the natural place for Christians to

come together to share all aspects of their lives, and again this is a tremendous witness to those who are round about. This is the model set out for us in Acts 2.46–7, where we read that the early believers 'broke bread in their homes and ate together with glad and sincere hearts, praising God and enjoying the favour of all the people. And the Lord added to their number daily those who were being saved'. Ronald Sider, in his minor classic, *Rich Christians in an Age of Hunger*,[7] emphasizes the link between this kind of unity and economic sharing, and evangelistic outreach. For those of us who lack the courage, in the midst of the affluent society with its insidious stereotyping, to live our lives in strict accordance with the model set out in the early chapters of Acts, then putting our homes at the disposal of God and of our fellow Christians may be at least a step in the right direction.

Other Uses of the Home

If I have dwelt mainly on fairly obvious, 'safe', uses of the home, it is because they are the ones with which I am myself most familiar. For a few people, however, a radical transformation of the home may be appropriate to their situation and the right change in direction. Supposing, for instance, you decide that you have a choice between seeking a new direction through a job outside the home and seeking one which is centred on the home full time, as it were. What sort of options might there be?

One possibility, despite all the warnings already mentioned, is to use your home for an extended household or even to house a community. If you belong to an active church you will probably have become aware of weaker members of the community who seem for one reason or another unable to cope with their current situation. These are perhaps obvious people to invite into your home for a while, in that you know them already and can expect support from other church members while they find their feet. Alternatively, you may feel particularly drawn to help those whose marriages are under strain, either offering them a place to come and think things through in peace, or giving them a temporary home if the marriage has already broken up. David Watson sets out the aim of such a venture, where extended households are formed with churches, as follows: 'To give a meaningful direction to the life of an individual and to make each person more aware of the needs of his neighbour.'[8] The dangers inherent in this ideal are clearly set out by Watson and others in various places, but the rewards must surely be considerable.

A second possibility, if it is appropriate to the life of the church in your area, is to allow your home to be used in the creation of a house church. According to David Prior these show the love of Jesus in a threefold way: 'love for the brethren, love for strangers and love for the under-privileged'.[9] In short, your home must function in precisely the same way as your (uninhabited) church building, but still remain a home, with all the qualities that we have already examined. This is clearly a tall order, but one which some are able to match up to.

Thirdly, in this trio of ideas, what about using the home for children? The need for adoptive parents may have diminished with the advent of the contraceptive pill and legalized abortion, but the call for foster parents is greater than ever, especially for parents who are prepared to take in 'difficult' or handicapped youngsters. This is clearly a full-time commitment which puts the existing home to particularly good use. Most people are by now aware that single or divorced people are no longer excluded from adopting and fostering, and there are many cases where the Social Services are looking for a home where the child will either be the only one or have much older brothers and sisters.

If a permanent arrangement is too much, it may instead be

appropriate for you to offer your home for holidays to a child or children from a deprived area. This only works if you live in the right place – perhaps in a seaside town or near countryside – but it can be immensely rewarding. Friends of mine have on several occasions let their garden be used as a camp site by children from an inner city area, some of whom had never seen a cow before their journey down. Your garden may not be up to this, but we can all appreciate the general idea and modify it to fit our own circumstances.

These three suggestions, and no doubt there are many other possibilities, all make big demands on the person concerned. Yet God could well be calling a divorced Christian to precisely this form of service in the home, and we overlook it at our peril.

There are two good reasons for thinking seriously about looking for a new direction at home. The first is related to a divorced person's attitude towards that home: what was once a delight can all too easily become a burden. Putting the home to use in God's service will not solve all the practical problems, but it will make it once again a source of joy and the problems will fall back into perspective. The second reason is concerned with individual circumstances. The home may be all that some people have to offer, and a lack of opportunities for service outside the home could mean that God is calling them to do just this. Whichever reason is the dominant one, the use of the home will not just be a source of much satisfaction to those who live there: what it may give to other people is immeasurable.

The house or flat does not have to be anything special: it is the love within it that counts. The Old Testament Wisdom literature has a number of picturesque ways of expressing this timeless truth, and non-vegetarians may like to ponder the following: 'Better a meal of vegetables where there is love than a fattened calf with hatred' (Prov. 15.17). I fear the saying may have lost something in translation, but even so, it still says it all.

FOR BIBLE READING AND PRAYER
Read Romans 12.1–16:

Therefore, I urge you, brothers, in view of God's mercy, to offer your bodies as living sacrifices, holy and pleasing to God – which is your spiritual act of worship. Do not conform any longer to the pattern of this world, but be transformed by the renewing of your mind. Then you will be able to test and approve what God's will is – his good, pleasing and perfect will.

For by the grace given me I say to every one of you: Do not think of yourself more highly than you ought, but rather think of yourself with sober judgment, in accordance with the measure of faith God has given you. Just as each of us has one body with many members, and these members do not all have the same function, so in Christ we who are many form one body, and each member belongs to all the others. We have different gifts, according to the grace given us. If a man's gift is prophesying, let him use it in proportion to his faith. If it is serving, let him serve; if it is teaching, let him teach; if it is encouraging, let him encourage; if it is contributing to the needs of others, let him give generously; if it is leadership, let him govern diligently; if it is showing mercy, let him do it cheerfully.

Love must be sincere. Hate what is evil; cling to what is good. Be devoted to one another in brotherly love. Honour one another above yourselves. Never be lacking in zeal, but keep your spiritual fervour, serving the Lord. Be joyful in hope, patient in affliction, faithful in prayer. Share with God's people who are in need. Practise hospitality.

Bless those who persecute you; bless and do not curse. Rejoice with those who rejoice; mourn with those who mourn. Live in harmony with one another. Do not be proud, but be willing to associate with people of low position. Do not be conceited.

Chapters 12 to 15 of Romans are devoted to ethical teaching, and it is significant that at the beginning of this passage Paul urges his readers to a complete and utter surrender to God. Once we are 'transformed by the renewing of [our] mind' we may start to discern God's will and with his help put it into practice.

Paul advocates a change of pattern in our life style, but note that this transformation nonetheless operates within the world itself. Paul is not calling us to withdraw from the world but to take a new direction within it. The theologian Karl Barth recommended to anyone seeking to understand the Epistle to the Romans 'a wide reading of contemporary secular literature – especially of newspapers!'[10]

We really have little choice about using what is given to us in the service of God, our possessions or our talents, because it is God who has given them to us in the first place. And the purpose of using them is to build up the Body of Christ, until, in the words of Ephesians 4.13, 'we all reach unity in the faith and in the knowledge of the Son of God, and become mature, attaining to the whole measure of the fullness of Christ'. We are not then to pride ourselves on our gifts; this is unnecessary because setting them to work will bring its own reward. Nor, indeed, are we to be jealous of the gifts given to others (cf. 1 Cor. 12.15–25), something which it is all too easy to do if you are tied to the house or are feeling a failure.

Instead we are to discover what responsibilities God is laying upon us and, having done so, carry them out well and unstintingly. This is part of the sacrifice that is talked about in the first verse: withholding nothing in ministering to one another. If we take this seriously it means placing ourselves and our homes at the disposal of the Christian community to which we belong as well as to those outside it.

It is perhaps only natural that Paul should back up his statements with a passage about love. It is impossible for a Christian to exercise his gifts of teaching, leadership, service and so on without also doing it in love. Notice, too, how a life of love points again and again to sharing the home. 'Practise hospitality,' says Paul, and at the end of the chapter (v.20) he quotes the Book of Proverbs: 'If your enemy is hungry, feed him; if he is thirsty, give him something to drink.'

The writer of the Epistle to the Hebrews makes the same connection: 'Keep on loving each others as brothers. Do not forget to entertain strangers, for by so doing some people have entertained angels without knowing it' (Heb. 13.1–2), while 1 Peter 4.9–10 not only echoes this command but also reminds us again of the reason why God gives us anything at all: 'Offer hospitality to one another without grumbling. Each one should use whatever gift he has received to serve others, faithfully administering God's grace in its various forms.'

Lord when we speak let us speak your words; when we serve let us serve in your strength. Teach us to use all that you have given us without reservation and in your service. Let us not value our possessions, our privacy, our gifts and abilities for their own sake, but help us to use them for you. That you may be praised in all things through Christ Jesus our Lord. Amen.

Give us, Almighty God, we pray, such a sense of all your mercies that our hearts may be unfeignedly thankful, and that we show forth your praise, not only with our lips but in our lives, by giving up ourselves to your service, and by walking before you in holiness and righteousness all our days; through Jesus Christ our Lord. Amen. (*Alternative Service Book, 1980, from the General Thanksgiving*)

Suggestions for further reading
John Perry, *Christian Leadership* (Hodder & Stoughton 1983) has a chapter entitled 'Leading in the home'. Ronald Sider's *Rich Christians in an Age of Hunger* (Hodder &

Stoughton 1978) should also be mentioned here, especially chapter 4, 'Economic relations among the people of God'. David Watson's autobiography, *You are my God* (Hodder & Stoughton 1983) has valuable observations on the topic of extended households.

References

1 D. Prior, *Bedrock, a Vision for the Local Church* (Hodder & Stoughton 1985), pp. 100, 101–2.
2 J. Woolmer, *Growing up to Salvation* (Triangle 1983), pp.79, 76.
3 J. Perry, *Christian Leadership* (Hodder & Stoughton 1983), p.41.
4 Ibid., p.95.
5 D. Watson, *I Believe in Evangelism* (Hodder & Stoughton 1976), p.100.
6 D. Watson, *Discipleship* (Hodder & Stoughton 1981), p.227.
7 R. Sider, *Rich Christians in an Age of Hunger* (Hodder & Stoughton 1978), see especially p.88ff.
8 D. Watson, *I Believe in the Church* (Hodder & Stoughton 1978), p.90.
9 *Bedrock,* p.102.
10. K. Barth, *The Epistle to the Romans,* tr. Hoskyns (Oxford University Press 1933), p.425.

5

New Directions at Work

Should you work at all? This first question is addressed particularly to women who have spent some or all of their married life at home. For others, both men and women, who are already in full- or part-time employment, the question is more likely to take the form 'Should I change my job?' or 'Should I give it up to care for my children?' That is something that people may only be able to answer through prayer and perhaps through the advice of those who know them and their circumstances well.

The immediate reason for seeking work, or, indeed, for changing jobs, may be financial, since few people actually gain financially by divorce or even end up in the same position as before. Statistics show that the majority of women, for example, face a substantial reduction in their standard of living. But starting work or changing jobs may be much more than a means of making more money: it can be the most obvious chance to do something different. New demands, new interests, new relationships and new situations are some of the possible results. For the housewife the chance to get out of the home and to escape from unhappy memories may be a pressing reason for seeking employment of some kind, however mundane.

Rising unemployment has of course meant that most people have had to revise their ideas about the sort of job (and salary!) they would like. 'Work' may well mean casual employment instead of a permanent post, payment by the hour instead of a monthly salary cheque, voluntary instead of paid. Perhaps this does not matter as much as it may appear to at first sight. Particularly important is the opportunity to look completely outside oneself and to set aside personal preoccupations through a change in surroundings.

Practical Needs

Looking for a Job

If you have not worked for some time you are in a very different position when looking for a job from a recent school- or college-leaver. It is a good idea to recognize this from the outset and not allow yourself to get despondent about your age or lack of formal qualifications, not least because these apparent 'minuses' may in the end turn out to be 'pluses'. In addition, not having careers advisers and contacts through school or college on hand, you will need to explore other ways of finding employment. You may have to think of ways of 'selling' yourself – no easy task if your self-confidence has already taken a few knocks.

A golden rule in job-hunting is, exploit your assets! For example, if you are older than the job descriptions are asking for, then think about the hidden advantages of that (there really are some!) and take confidence from them. You will have picked up all kinds of experience that a school-leaver knows nothing about, from dealing with businesses, workmen and deliverymen to being a good cook or a good organizer. Bear in mind, too, that many employers will be interested in taking on someone older who is reliable, likely to stay in the area and with the motivation to stick with the job. It may help to make out a list of everything you see as a possible advantage, both to boost your own confidence and to help sort out what kind of job you should be looking for. Be open to whatever comes up, whether or not it is the type of work you originally trained for.

A great advantage most people will have over the average school-leaver is access to a wide range of friends and acquaintances, in short, 'contacts' – so use them! There is no point in being shy about making your needs known; necessity will probably win the day over shyness in the end anyway. Let your friends know that you are hoping to get a job and that you are willing to be flexible. Remember too that within your own church there will be many people whose social and business 'contacts' are quite different from yours, and it is surprising how many jobs seem to get filled through this kind of grapevine. Your fellow Christians may be very willing to help in this way; however, this is not to say that you should pester the local GP to take you on as his receptionist just because he also happens to be the church-warden!

Many churches will let you put an advertisement in their monthly magazine or weekly bulletin, and it is worth asking other churches in your area to do this if your own congregation cannot help. If you want to look further afield, try advertising in the church press. After all, it is common sense to look for a job where your Christian commitment will stand you in good stead and one which might also lead you further on in God's service.

Even so, job-hunting can be a depressing experience. Not only do the rejections have a habit of piling up, but there will always be somebody ready to tell you that you need not or ought not to work anyway. When that happens you will need to fall back on your assurance of God's will for your life. Remember that God will provide when his time is right and in retrospect you will find that this is very obvious. Do not be afraid to pray over such specific, practical matters. You may find it helpful to recall the concern Paul showed in his letters for the very practical, everyday matters that preoccupied the early Church. When Paul thanks the Philippians for the welcome gifts they had sent him he adds: 'My God will supply every need of yours according to his riches in glory in Christ Jesus' (Phil. 4.19 RSV).

Retraining

Looking for a job may be a matter of financial necessity, or a personal challenge, or both. For the same reasons it may seem sensible to undertake some form of retraining. You may even feel that now is a good time to realize some long-held private ambition in this respect. There is no shortage of courses on offer; it is for you to decide what best suits your interests, your availability and your pocket.

First of all it is a good idea to take the time to obtain details of courses available at every level in the subjects that interest you. You may decide that evening classes are the most suitable, in which case your local library will have full details. If you are more ambitious you might want to consider a full-time course at a polytechnic, university or college of education. If you did not benefit from a student grant when you were younger you would do well to find out from the local education authority whether you qualify for one now. Alternatively, family commitments may make a correspondence course or Open University course a more viable option.

If you decide on any of these you will find that the demands made upon your time and energy will be high, but this is balanced by the fact that you will to some extent be in a position to arrange your own timetable. If you have suffered from loneliness in the past you may be surprised to find that the time will come when you long for an evening on your own again with nothing to do!

As in other areas it is vital to recognize your own gifts and limitations. If you have never been good at studying alone, then now is not the time to try again – go along to classes with other people instead. If you are totally unartistic try not to be tempted by courses in typography or fashion design. On the other hand it is sensible to catch up on what has been going on since you last worked. A course in word-processing or basic computing will stand you in good stead in a surprisingly wide range of jobs.

Whatever you may decide on, it is essential that you choose something you really want to do, even if you have so far lacked the confidence to try. Very often other people can discern our gifts (or potential ones) better than we can ourselves, so do not be too shy to seek advice from friends. And remember that our gifts change in the course of our lives, and also that even the apparently least significant abilities are God-given. I find it very reassuring that Paul, in the description of the Body of Christ in 1 Corinthians 12, includes alongside the apostles and prophets, 'those able to help others' and 'those with gifts of administration' (1 Cor. 12.28). All too often the Church, to say nothing of the world, sets great store by spectacular gifts and fails to give equal regard to those whose job it is simply to care for others day by day or to keep wheels turning. Seek to identify your gifts, then, and set them to work, making use of whatever help and training resources are at your disposal.

Flexibility

If you are a single parent looking for a job you will probably be hoping for work which offers maximum flexibility, so that you can accommodate both job and children satisfactorily. It would be wrong to give the impression that the two go together easily. It is also unfortunate that, if you do not have a resident granny, the type of employment that best fits family commitments almost always presupposes a high degree of training (e.g. teaching) or talent (so that you are in a position to dictate your own terms). Even then, many working mothers in male-dominated professions, for example, feel they have to bend over backwards to avoid giving their children's needs as a reason for lateness or absence.

Happily the last couple of decades have seen considerable changes in social attitudes to working mothers (and fathers) and a growing recognition that many women need job satisfaction outside the home, whatever their marital status. One of the more fruitful consequences of this has been the steadily increasing practice of job sharing. Some advertisements will say that job sharers are welcome. If they do not, then it is worth teaming up with a friend and approaching potential employers together. Obviously such an arrangement needs to be thought through very carefully first and all kinds of questions and implications need to be faced (e.g. Can you bear the thought of looking after each other's children? What about holidays?) And when you have done that you will have to convince an employer that it will work from his or her point of view as well as from yours.

If job sharing is not possible and you do not come into the resident granny category, all is not lost. Many jobs fit neatly into the school day if you are prepared to work through the lunch hour, or to settle for a less than full-time position. Alternatively, it is often possible to take turns with other parents on the school run. You may even find someone who is willing to look after a child after school on a regular basis to help you out.

There are many ways of making arrangements for children that will work perfectly well provided that the children keep to some sort of routine and know what to expect. Personally I have always tried to avoid having to get someone to take care of my children at both ends of the school day. For me this means that an early (or late) start to the working day is balanced by an early (or late) finish, and there have been very few occasions indeed when this has not been possible, however demanding the job in question. Others will want to set their own rules. Remember that most children are extraordinarily adaptable and will slot very happily into a new routine, provided that it does indeed have some recognizable order to it.

There are also, now, a number of self-help neighbourhood groups springing up around the country. Such groups pool their resources in order to encourage and enable single parents to seek work or undertake training. If there is not such a group in your area, why not think about setting one up?

In many ways, working from home may be a most attractive option. The growing number of people registered as self-employed almost certainly includes many single parents who have adapted both their home and working lives to fit their situation. Working from home offers many advantages and the tax benefits of doing so should not be overlooked either (see Appendix). Depending, of course, on your line of work, self-employment can be an exciting and challenging new direction to take.

The first prerequisite is a place to work. While some dedicated souls may be able to run a profitable business from their kitchen tables, I suspect most of us need a room set aside, if only to retreat to when the house resounds to pop music over half-term. An extra room is not as extravagant as it sounds, for again it attracts income-tax concessions. And if there is nowhere else to go, there may be some therapeutic value in reordering a double bedroom as an office-cum-bedsit which is decorated according to your own taste and no one else's!

Initially a certain amount of expense is almost inevitable, although your bank manager may be sympathetic to the idea of a loan if you are a long-standing customer or can convince him of your ability to make a profit! You may also need the services of an accountant if you are not familiar with all the intricacies of the tax system or feel unable to manage financial affairs of any complexity. Even so, it should be possible to start modestly and allow things to develop at their own pace.

There are still a few drawbacks to this happy state of affairs. If you are used to working with a lot of other people around you will undoubtedly miss this basic human contact or stimulation. The converse of this problem is that most people have no qualms about interrupting your working day at home with phone calls, visits, invitations to coffee and so on. Handling this again is something that you need to work out for yourself, but whatever you decide stick to it, or no one will know where they stand. My own practice when working at home has usually been to restrict purely social activities to lunch hours, but to welcome phone calls as a safeguard against isolation (although at times of pressure the answerphone goes on!). Similarly, children need to know quite unambiguously the times at which you can legitimately be disturbed and those when you are working, just as if you were in an office on the other side of town. Make it clear exactly when you will be free for them and try to keep to it.

What job? What training? Where? When? – these are all practical questions which individuals will have to answer in their own way on the basis of their own needs and environment. But to provide these answers is not the end of the story. To seek new directions through work is also to enter a new situation actively and willingly, and the consequences may be far-reaching.

Spiritual Growth

The story of Paul in Corinth in Acts 18 gives us an interesting insight into the way in which the great evangelist worked. We are told that Paul went to see Aquila and Priscilla who, with other Jews, had been driven out of Italy by Claudius, and 'because [Paul] was a tentmaker as they were, he stayed and worked with them. Every Sabbath he reasoned in the synagogue, trying to persuade Jews and Greeks' (Acts 18.3–4). From this we see first that Paul makes friends through his trade – his work is an important point of contact with other people. Secondly, Paul himself works in Corinth; we can assume that he did so both to be self-supporting and in order to meet people. His preaching activities for the time being are restricted to one day a week. We have already touched on the role of Priscilla and Aquila in the previous chapter, and their gifts of hospitality and home-based evangelism. There are many Christians for whom the home is the centre of their ministry; there are others whose particular gifts lead them outside the home. Both forms of ministry are, of course, equally valid and should be held in mutual respect.

For most of us it is at our place of work that our involvement with affairs of the world is greatest; where our friends and colleagues are non-Christians and where we become most acutely aware of the needs and suffering in society. Quite obviously there are exceptions to this. I know of one elderly Christian who is able to pray wholeheartedly for the needs of the world as she perceives them via her television and newspapers and through her visitors; I am sure that her prayer life in this respect is much richer than that of many of us who have the advantage of experiencing society at first hand through our work.

It is at work again that we are most likely to encounter unpopularity just by virtue of the fact of being a Christian, and equally it is at work that our Christian values and beliefs are most put to the test. It seems to me that the working life of any Christian involves decisions about (a) involvement in society and (b) personal witness and lifestyle. Both of these represent a challenge for anyone seeking new directions and in each case being a Christian who is divorced is far from irrelevant.

(a) Involvement in Society

It is increasingly apparent in Britain in the 1980s that society does not welcome Christian involvement. Statements by church leaders on such topics as unemployment and inner-city deprivation have been met with anger and abuse by politicians. Yet there is no shortage of biblical examples to justify such involvement. The great leaders and prophets of the Old Testament protested against social oppression and suffered accordingly, while in the New Testament we see that spiritual commitment to the gospel of Christ can hardly be separated from its social consequences. Yet there are also Christians who frown at the Church's 'interference' in politics but, as Michael Green puts it, 'Unless religion does interfere in politics, God help politics'.[1]

This may seem a trifle remote from our everyday working lives in an office, classroom or factory. But social concern is not the sole prerogative of natural leaders and speech-makers; it is the right and duty of every Christian both to talk and to act in such matters, and he or she will not be thanked for doing so. Michael Green goes on: 'The Christian will not merely protest about the abuses in society. He will get involved in society and work for their removal . . . The devil has got to be resisted, not merely deprecated.'[2]

At the risk of sounding cynical, there can be few areas of employment where such abuses are not evident if we care to look for them. Industrial unrest, exploitation, unjust pay structures and a host of other problems suddenly cease to be items we choose to ignore in the newspapers when we find ourselves working alongside them.

Now all Christians who are *in* the world (without being *of* the world) feel acutely the suffering of their fellow human beings. You do not, of course, have to be a Christian to be moved to tears by television pictures of starving children. But Christian grief has an extra dimension: those who are being denied food by a selfish world are God's children; yet man's greed turns him daily away from God's will for his people. So Christians are vulnerable because in trying to share God's love they lay themselves open to hurt and rejection. Jesus gave his disciples clear warning of this: 'If you belonged to the world, it would love you as its own. As it is, you do not belong to the world, but I have chosen you out of the world. That is why the world hates you' (John 15.19).

If I seem to have laboured this point it is because I believe it is essential that a committed Christian who has also been through the trauma of divorce should not be under any illusions as to what is implied by being in the world. Are you prepared for *further* suffering, albeit of a different kind? Do you regard it as a challenge? If so, then my next question must be, what difference does divorce make?

At first sight it may seem to make no difference at all. There have been times when I have found it comforting to work among people who show no surprise or shock at divorce, particularly when the going has been less than easy in Christian circles. In retrospect, however, I can see that this was surely wrong. My colleagues were not shocked because they did not share any Christian expectations of marriage. For the sake of my own comfort I had fallen into the trap of appreciating the world's values: I had become 'of the world'. To move outside the circle of home and church, then, is to expose oneself deliberately to spiritual temptation and to further suffering. Yet this is the way of the Christian, to whom Jesus's promise still holds good: 'I have told you these things so that in me you may have peace. In this world you will have trouble. But take heart! I have overcome the world' (John 16.33).

At work, as in any other situation, people who know you are divorced will recognize that you have experienced a certain degree of suffering, and this will draw others in need to you. As we saw in chapter 2, that puts you in a very privileged position, and such opportunities for Christian witness as well as for practical caring are not to be missed. It is interesting how even the most hardened atheist is prepared to confide in a Christian colleague in times of trouble, in the hope of finding sympathy and compassion, and we should not shrink from displaying a Christ-like love to such people. But in so doing we must face up to the fact that this will usually be at some cost to ourselves, for once the need for love is past it will readily be replaced by resentment at

92

having displayed weakness and a renewed desire to inflict hurt.

(b) Personal Witness and Lifestyle

It is at work that the contrast between Christians and non-Christians is most marked; so far as home-life is concerned there will be many values pertaining to family life and other relationships that will be common to both groups. It is at work that the Christian encounters the real world head on – a world which is still much preached about in churches by people with little experience of it. Here the Christian will be judged by his or her actions and relationships; but the relationships will be in a quite different category from those experienced within a church fellowship, where the closeness can, as David Prior admits,[3] verge on the oppressive; and the actions will be very much more complex than those which we allow our fellow-Christians to observe in a church setting.

At work people will look at a divorced Christian and see someone who has been through an experience which is all too familiar in the world and yet who has come through it in a way that is not familiar. This is a natural starting point for witness and evangelism, and an easy one since the initiative is likely to come from someone else. People will be anxious to know how you coped; one or two will be curious to know what your position is in the church as a result. Be prepared to tell them!

How often we let this opportunity slip away. If we reply along the lines that our church has been very supportive, true though this may be, the questioner is left feeling vaguely dissatisfied and possibly jealous of what he sees as being denied to non-members. He will find it a poor explanation for any resilience or inner peace that we may exhibit and go off muttering about the cliquishness of the local church.

When God and our fellow Christians have guided us through the pain of divorce, surrounded us with love and led us to increased spiritual maturity through the experience, we really have no choice but to tell the world about it. A glowing testimony to church 'help' or the vicar's visiting is not enough; we have to go to what lies behind these actions – the love of God and the gospel message.

In his book *I Believe in Evangelism* David Watson draws attention to the curiosity which any personal testimony to experience of Christ will arouse in others.[4] This is surely the most basic contribution a Christian can make at work to the Church's task of evangelism. Nonetheless it would be wrong to suppose that everyone finds this equally easy. We are not all called to be evangelists, in the way that leaders such as Billy Graham and David Watson are called. But we are not permitted to be reticent either, since we are told that the Holy Spirit will give us courage for even the simplest confession of faith.

The prayer of the believers in Jerusalem in Acts 4 is very simple: 'Now Lord, . . . enable your servants to speak your word with great boldness' (Acts 4.29). This should be our prayer too, always bearing in mind that the result may be dramatic: 'After they prayed, the place where they were meeting was shaken. And they were all filled with the Holy Spirit and spoke the word of God boldly' (4.31).

David Watson also mentions integrity, which we must see here as a further form of witness at work. In 2 Corinthians 4 Paul emphasizes the truth of his message in the face of the world's dishonesty. Consequently, he says, 'We are hard pressed on every side, but not crushed; perplexed, but not in despair; persecuted, but not abandoned; struck down, but not destroyed' (2 Cor. 4.8–9). So it is for divorced Christians who have suffered in a way that non-Christians may readily identify with, but who have not reacted as many non-Christians might. Integrity of lifestyle involves demonstrating that it is possible to live a peaceful and fulfilled life after divorce, without engaging in wrong or unsuitable personal relationships, without threatening other people's marriages, without hatred or bitterness, and without abandoning children and home.

Finally, despite what I have already said about testifying to God rather than to people, the divorced Christian is well placed to bear witness to Christian love in action. In David Watson's words:

> Today it is the Body of Christ, when deeply united in love, and not individual Christians, that can most of all make people hungry for God. There is an infectious happiness in Christians who really love one another as well as loving Christ . . . ; this gives rise to natural opportunities of sharing our faith in Christ with those who have seen and felt something attractive which they have not experienced before.[5]

There are these three things, then – personal testimony, integrity of lifestyle and Christian love – that the divorced Christian is supremely well placed to put across in the course of his or her work. It will not always be easy to do, but with prayer it will never be impossible. And whatever the outcome it is certain that the person who bears witness in this way will benefit greatly as a result and be further encouraged in the Christian life.

In seeking new directions at work, the divorced Christian is doing two things. On one level he or she may be making a personal advance in meeting new challenges and in coping with a changed situation. Simultaneously, however, it is also a spiritual advance in confronting the world and taking up the challenge of evangelism. So what may have begun as financial necessity or psychological desirability can result in a positive area for spiritual growth. Do not, therefore, if you are in a position to choose, rush to dismiss the possibility of employment in favour of some more 'godly' occupation. The opportunities may at first sight appear modest, but the potential is enormous.

FOR BIBLE READING AND PRAYER
Read 2 Corinthians 5.17 — 6.10:

Therefore, if anyone is in Christ, he is a new creation; the old has gone, the new has come! All this is from God, who reconciled us to himself through Christ and gave us the ministry of reconciliation: that God was reconciling the world to himself in Christ, not counting men's sins against them. And he has committed to us the message of reconciliation.

We are therefore Christ's ambassadors, as though God were making his appeal through us. We implore you on Christ's behalf: Be reconciled to God. God made him who had no sin to be a sin offering for us, so that in him we might become the righteousness of God.

As God's fellow-workers we urge you not to receive God's grace in vain. For he says,

'In the time of my favour I heard you,
    and in the day of salvation I helped you.'

I tell you, now is the time of God's favour, now is the day of salvation.

We put no stumbling-block in anyone's path, so that our ministry will not be discredited. Rather, as servants of God we commend ourselves in every way: in great endurance; in troubles, hardships and distresses; in beatings, imprisonments and riots; in hard work, sleepless nights and hunger; in purity, understanding, patience and kindness; in the Holy Spirit and in sincere love; in truthful speech and in the power of God; with weapons of righteousness in the right hand and in the left; through glory and dishonour, bad report and good report; genuine, yet regarded as impostors; known, yet regarded as unknown; dying, and yet we live on; beaten and yet not killed; sorrowful, yet always rejoicing; poor, yet making many rich; having nothing, and yet possessing everything.

The context of the early verses in this passage is Paul's discussion of Christ's death and its significance for us. Quite simply it is 'life-transforming'. It heals the broken relationship between God and man. But it goes beyond that in that as a direct consequence it lays upon us the responsibility to continue that work of healing, of 'reconciliation'. Paul describes us as 'Christ's ambassadors' (the Greek text says 'we minister on behalf of Christ') – the vehicles, however imperfect, for God's message. This is not then a passive relationship: it involves hard work and is a great responsibility, as the Greek suggests. Similarly, we are described both as God's fellow-workers and as servants, and the hardships of such a ministry are graphically spelt out, from Paul's own experience.

Though we may not share all Paul's hardships, the qualities he lists are not a bad picture of today's Christians in their work in the world, singling out as they do the Christian values which the world undervalues and the conflicting reactions of the world.

Yet there is no suggestion that Christian service should be undertaken anywhere other than in the world, that is in the thick of contemporary, secular society. This too is the teaching of Jesus. Compare, for example, Matthew 5.13–16, where Jesus describes his followers as 'the salt of the earth' and 'the light of the world', ending with the exhortation 'let your light shine before men that they may see your good deeds and praise your Father in heaven'. Jesus sends his disciples out into the world, ill-equipped in secular terms, on a seemingly impossible task ('I am sending you out like sheep among wolves' – Matt. 10.16) but with the promise that 'you will be given what to say, for it will not be you speaking, but the Spirit of your Father speaking through you' (Matt. 10.19–20).

Through Christ's death on the cross we are healed; as a result we are sent out by God on this same task of reconciliation and we enjoy his protection as we do his will.

Send us out, Lord, in the power of your Spirit, to live and work to your praise and glory. Amen. (*Alternative Service Book, 1980*)

Suggestions for further reading
Wendy Green, *The Future of the Family* (Mowbray 1984) has a short section on 'Women and work', as well as chapters on divorce, one-parent families and remarriage. On evangelism see especially chapter 6 of *I Believe in Evangelism* by David Watson (Hodder & Stoughton 1976), entitled 'Personal Evangelism. D. Bleakley's *In Place of Work . . . the Sufficient Society* (SCM 1981) is a study of the role of the churches and the Christian community at a time of industrial change and new technology.

References

1 M. Green, *I Believe in Satan's Downfall* (Hodder & Stoughton 1981), p.240.
2 ibid., p.244.
3 D. Prior, *The Suffering and the Glory* (Hodder & Stoughton 1985), p.137. 'A kind of interpersonal claustrophobia has begun to afflict many Christians, especially after they have experienced oppressive closeness in relationships in a given church-fellowship.'
4 D. Watson, *I Believe in Evangelism* (Hodder & Stoughton 1976), ch. 6 'Personal Evangelism'.
5 ibid., p.105.

6

New Directions at Church

Here at last we have come to the crunch! What is the role of a divorced Christian in the Church? Normally if someone breaks the rules of a society or community to which he or she belongs, the natural reaction of that society is to expel the offending member. This preserves the integrity of the whole and is seen as setting an example to the rest. But by definition the Christian Church cannot cast out such people. The Church exists for sinners to be saved, not for the perfect to become yet more perfect. Nowadays this is generally recognized, and while some schools of Christian thought will require offenders to carry out some form of penance, in principle forgiveness is on offer. But – and this is the real crux of the matter – to what extent is forgiveness to be equated with integration?

In these last two chapters we shall be looking at the way in which the Church translates theoretical forgiveness into terms of actual acceptance and encouragement. I shall leave to the final chapter the variety of attitudes within the Church on the doctrinal issues surrounding the acceptance of divorce and remarriage. First, we have to consider more practical matters, in particular the position of a divorced Christian who wants to use his or her experience as a basis for seeking new directions within the life of the Church.

I have already, in chapter 3, hinted at the paradox that confronts a divorced Christian. With sympathetic help and encouragement it should be possible for such a person to turn past suffering to good account and to lead an enriched Christian life in the context of either the home or work or both. However, if the pain of divorce is indeed to lead to a better knowledge of God and a deeper commitment to his work, then the Church is an obvious place in which to express such a commitment. It is a natural place to seek a new direction, but probably also the most difficult one. It is perhaps only within the Church that a Christian will experience opposition and even hostility because of being divorced (particularly if he or she has or seeks a role of ministry), a situation which society in general would regard as unacceptable.

In addition, and even more crucial, is the fact that for anyone actively to seek service in this way is to engage in spiritual warfare. For someone who is divorced there is no doubt that this is a point of vulnerability which the devil will not be slow to attack in many different ways.

Before considering the practical possibilities of new directions at church, therefore, it is essential that we first face up to some of the spiritual questions that go with them.

Spiritual Questions

Rejection

It seems to me that spiritual rejection – as distinct from the feelings of inadequacy mentioned in chapter 1 – can take two distinct forms, which are roughly akin to two attitudes towards divorce in the Church today.

In my own experience, and in the experience of many others, the attitude of most Christians is a marvellously warm and accepting one. Indeed, the support that I and others have been given (in my own case by an evangelical congregation in particular) has been so strong that it seems niggardly to talk about rejection at all. Yet, until one is completely at peace with God, human acceptance will never totally quench the lurking fear of God's rejection. It may be, therefore, that a church which does not normally encourage the practice of confession is perhaps leaving one part of the healing process incomplete.

There are, of course, alternatives to formal confession to cope with this particular fear of rejection. I am thinking notably of the laying on of hands which for me personally assured me of God's acceptance. Another possibility might be praying for spiritual healing with another person, who might well be a leader in the church or a Christian whose spiritual maturity is evident.

The other side of the coin is to be seen in churches where the emphasis on confession and absolution is so great that human acceptance appears to be withheld until this hurdle – and possibly others as well – has been cleared. It is, I think, important to realize, first that confession on its own, without human encouragement, is not enough for most of us. It is never easy, for example, to pursue a course of action which you know to be God's will in the face of human opposition. How much harder is it, then, to accept the fact of God's forgiveness when other *Christians* – not the world at large – are by their attitudes suggesting that this is not the case and are denying divorced Christians their support and encouragement.

Secondly, I do not think that Christians who are separated or divorced should be left in a kind of spiritual limbo until it is felt that they can decently be accepted back into the Christian fellowship. I cannot accept the suggestion made by David Phypers[1] that divorced Christians who remarry should find that their integration into a new congregation is dependent on a sort of congregational vote after a probationary period.

A divorced Christian, therefore, may experience feelings of rejection by God or by man, and will need to be reassured both of God's forgiveness and of the acceptance of that forgiveness by his or her fellow Christians. If there is any doubt as to either, it will be very hard to continue and grow in the Christian life, let alone take an active part in Christian service.

I recently went to preach in a small country church and was somewhat surprised to be told by a committed member of the congregation that her husband (who did not normally attend anyway) would refuse to come on this occasion if a woman preached the sermon. In his mind, apparently, this ranked as 'unconventional' and was therefore unacceptable. (In the event the husband did come and studiously read his hymnbook all the time I was speaking!) Now I do not think this person knew, or cared, that I was divorced. His prejudice was simply one against women having any kind of leadership role in the church, and as such I did not feel inclined to treat it too seriously, particularly since it came from someone who was to all intents and purposes outside the church. In any case, since I was leading a local mission, it would have been decidedly odd if I had not preached at a main service.

There are, however, other forms of prejudice, and other types of prejudiced people, that are not to be dismissed so lightly. If, for instance, in that same situation, one of the committed Christians in the church had objected to me not as a woman but as a divorcee, then I should have felt bound to take that objection very seriously indeed. Of course such opposition is hurtful, but if it stems from genuine conviction it ought not to be personal. Which means that given sufficient love and patience it should in the end be possible to work through it on a personal basis. I know of a number of Christians who are in a position of leadership or otherwise active in their own churches whose personal circumstances are unknown to most of the people they are working with. In the end it is their own witness to the presence of God in their lives which prevails, and general prejudices become irrelevant.

What I should like to say to any divorced Christian seeking an active role in the Church is not only that you may be hurt but also be aware that unwittingly you may be hurting others. However, once you can show that you are sensitive to this you are well on the way to removing it.

Resilience

'We all tend to be a bit paranoid,' a divorced clergyman told me, and that is undoubtedly true. We imagine rejection where none exists and hurt ourselves as a result. This is one extreme – to imagine that a project in the church meets with hostility because I, as a divorced Christian, am involved. The other extreme is arrogance – the assumption that it cannot possibly be anything to do with me. Obviously it is desirable to look for the happy medium, and again it seems that both openness and humility before God and the encouragement and support of other Christians are essential in order to strike a balance.

In embarking on new directions in the Church it is right, I believe, to pray for resilience once you are sure that God is calling you to work in this way, however menial that work may be. It cannot be the case that God intends those whose marriages have failed to drop out of his service, particularly if they have special gifts to offer. On the other hand, I cannot agree with David Phypers' suggestion[2] that those who are divorced should seek some form of Christian service as an alternative to remarriage! God calls each of us in his own way according to our gifts and capabilities, and Christian service is neither a consolation prize for the unmarried nor an unattainable goal for the divorced. God does not reject us nor our desire to serve him because of what we have done wrong; as the writer to the Hebrews put it, 'let us also lay aside every weight, and sin which clings so closely, and let us run with perseverance the race that is set before us' (Heb. 12.1, RSV). The same writer also reminds us: 'You have need of endurance, so that you may do the will of God and receive what is promised' (Heb. 10.36, RSV).

I have already made the point that to embark on Christian service is to engage in spiritual warfare. Inevitably the devil will try to use separation, divorce or remarriage to create opposition and division within the Church, to undermine a particular person's gifts or ministry. It is crucial therefore to recognize that feelings of hurt and inadequacy may not always spring just from personal humility; such feelings may be directly contrary to the will of God. Michael Green writes powerfully against defeatism in the Church[3] and we would all do well to examine ourselves in this respect, remembering the rhetorical question in 1 John: 'Who is it that overcomes the world but he who believes that Jesus is the Son of God?' (1 John 5.5).

A further need for God-given resilience stems from the loneliness that is inherent in Christian leadership. Again this is an area where someone who has experienced the loneliness of marital breakdown is liable to be hurt unless he or she is prepared for it. In *Christian Leadership* John Perry includes this cost of leadership alongside criticism, suffering and discouragement, and the divorced Christian is perhaps more prone than most to all of these things. As the author points out,[4] loneliness in leadership can be self-inflicted and it is not only foolish but unscriptural to ignore the support offered by others. On the other hand, it is not easy to go home from, say, a meeting or church service where much has been asked of you and have only the dog to talk to! I have at times detected a tendency in myself to over-react to what others have said or done, simply because there has been no means of unwinding, no one at home to provide a more objective point of view.

Paul, at the end of his second letter to Timothy, acknowledges both the loneliness and its solution:

At my first defence no one took my part; all deserted me. May it not be charged against them! But the Lord stood by me and gave me strength to proclaim the message fully, that all the Gentiles might hear it. So I was rescued from the lion's mouth. The Lord will rescue me from every evil and save me for his heavenly kingdom. (2 Tim. 4.16–18, RSV)

So it will be for all of us, whatever our circumstances, when we stick our necks out to do God's work – he will give us resilience on earth, and a place in his Kingdom.

Prayer

The Body of Christ can do nothing unless it is rooted in prayer. This is, of course, true for all Christians in all aspects of our daily lives. But it is in our service to God, as members of that Body, that we need not depend solely on our own prayers. It is our right to expect the prayer support of the other members just as it is their right to count on it from us.

This obligation is one that Paul made particularly clear to the early Church, and he used strong language to do so. In 2 Corinthians 1.11 we read: 'You also *must* help us by prayer, so that many will give thanks on our behalf for the blessing granted us in answer to many prayers.' The apostle does not see this as an easy thing: 'I appeal to you, brethren, by our Lord Jesus Christ and by the love of the Spirit, to *strive* together with me in your prayers on my behalf . . .' (Rom. 15.30, RSV), but he has confidence in its effectiveness: 'I *know* that through your prayers and the help of the Spirit of Jesus Christ this will turn out for my deliverance' (Phil. 1.19, RSV) (my italics).

It is, therefore, a matter for encouragement and for rejoicing that whatever tasks we may undertake in our church, from cleaning the floor to preaching a sermon, the other members of the church will be praying for us. It is encouraging and vital, for, as I have already suggested, it is in this overt form of Christian service that we particularly attract the attention of the forces of evil. If you have any doubts about this, look at the spiritual battles fought by churches that have embarked on building programmes to improve and increase their work in evangelism and worship, and you will see how Satan attacks individuals who openly offer service to God, however, insignificant their role may seem to be.[5]

Most churches will have their own ways of supporting their members in prayer, through organized prayer groups, house groups, monthly magazines and so on. If you decide to follow some new direction of service in the church, make sure you ask for prayer from the appropriate quarter.

In addition, there has quite recently come into being a fellowship which specifically offers prayer support to those who have been hurt or feel rejected in Christian circles through divorce, separation or remarriage. This is the Magdalene Fellowship (see Appendix) which aims to draw together Christians who have suffered in this way and others who wish to pray for them and encourage them to grow in their Christian life. The Fellowship was started by a couple who had experienced rejection by many Christians and then found more and more people with similar experiences. The belief that growth in Christ is not something which is denied to separated, divorced or remarried Christians underlies the work of the group, which extends nationwide.

Whatever channels we use, we need to join our prayers with those of others, whether these are the prayers of the whole church, a small group, or others in a similar situation. Through such prayer we will indeed be able to undertake the tasks laid upon us in the church and receive great encouragement in our performance of them.

Practical Possibilities

Gifts

What can I do? This is a question which naturally is asked by all Christians, not just the divorced, and the answers can equally apply to everyone. However, the question as asked by a divorced Christian has two less common aspects to it. In the first place it is being asked by someone who has suffered, has overcome and wants to offer that whole experience back to God. Or, to put it another way, it is being asked by someone who may appear weak and disadvantaged in the eyes of society but who has found strength in God. The Christian fellowship needs to recognize this and take advantage of it.

Secondly, on a more mundane level, divorced Christians may be in a slightly different position from other church members in what they have to offer, and often it will also be doing him or her a service to have an offer of help or involvement taken up. This is particularly true when there is an obvious personal gap to be filled, for example at the end of the working day when there is no one to come home to, or at weekends or holidays when children may be visiting the other parent. In practice this can mean availability at unusual times when other help is hard to find, for example hospital visiting around Christmas time, offering hospitality, babysitting and a hundred-and-one other things. Wise church leaders will be alert to the lifestyle of the divorced Christians in their congregation and will suggest forms of service which are compatible with their availability and own needs.

Nonetheless the basic question remains, What can I do? At a guess, the majority of people in any congregation need constantly to be reminded that they each have something of value to offer the church and the community, and need encouragement to go ahead and do it. Everyone is good at something. Some people may be obviously talented at a depressingly large number of things; others will not admit to any talents at all. And a few have the gift of seeking out the talents of others, overcoming their reticence and encouraging them to use their gifts.

'Gifts' and 'talents' are big words, but they are not reserved for clever things and clever people. The world would be an impossible place if it were just full of highly talented people in the traditional sense of the word. The idea that we and our various gifts are all needed to make up the Body of Christ is a theme that Paul returns to several times; read Romans 12.3–8, 1 Corinthians 12.27ff. and Ephesians 4.1–16. Just as most people are not going to be great artists or politicians, so most Christians are not going to be outstanding teachers or spiritual leaders. We have already seen that Paul includes the often neglected (even despised) administrators in his list of those given a specific role within the Church in accordance with their gifts (1 Cor. 12.28). Another example might be the gift of hospitality, which many people do not see as a gift, but which is mentioned twice in the New Testament precisely in this context (in Romans 12.13 and 1 Peter 4.9).

Whatever our gifts prove to be – practical or intellectual, pastoral or spiritual – let us not forget the injunction in Romans 12.6: 'Having gifts that differ according to the grace given to us, let us use them.'

Service in the Local Church

Supposing you want to offer your gifts to your local church, how do you go about it? There will of course (in any normal church!) be regular requests for specific things – people to distribute cards or magazines, to provide food for parish events, to arrange flowers, sing in the choir and so on. On the face of it, however, this may be more of a discouragement to the uninvolved lay person than an encouragement. When you know that your own flowers always fall out of their vases, that everyone else's flans taste better than yours, and that the choir would not really relish your indifferent voice, what then? I think it is important to have the imagination to see beyond the immediate task. For example, I have heard of someone who was given what appeared to be a routine task of updating the church electoral roll but who turned it into a real challenge by visiting and praying for various people on it. If you are given a pile of magazines to put through letterboxes why not knock on a few doors and see what develops.

Another point to bear in mind is not to be limited by existing church structures. You do not have to wait for the vicar to form a maintenance team before putting your do-it-yourself skills at his disposal. If they are looking for an organist and you play the flute, then let people see what a marvellous accompaniment a piano and flute can be for some of the more meditative hymns. In short, whatever you can do, offer it to the church. Equally, let others help you to discover new gifts. Until you try you may never know how well you can organize a fund-raising event, read a lesson or teach a Sunday School class. And if you find you can't – well you won't have to do it again!

Prayer

If, however, you find yourself very restricted in what you can offer the church – perhaps because of the demands of work or of a young family – what then? Is there any way in which you can offer yourself to the church family?

A few years ago my own church issued each member of the congregation with a 'talents register' – a formidable three-page document listing all kinds of gifts and areas of service which people were invited to tick and return. Their offers were then taken up by the clergy or appropriate church officers as the occasion demanded. Now this register contained an item entitled 'Time to pray – specific prayer requests will be sent to you from time to time.' Interestingly enough only a very small proportion of people ticked that – perhaps because many of us recognized that it was not so much the lack of time but the lack of will to find it that was the problem. Nonetheless this is perhaps the most useful function anyone can be called upon to carry out, and one which is entirely compatible with, say, travelling to and from the shops or office. Many churches will have existing channels whereby prayer needs are swiftly communicated to their members. If yours does not have this, create your own by asking people (clergy, lay officers, missionary representatives etc) what they would like you to pray for and let them know that you are continuing to do it. You may want to ask one or two others to join you and a whole scheme of prayer partners may evolve from it. But whatever form it takes, prayer for the church will always be needed and always be an effective form of service.

Beyond Parish Boundaries

It is sometimes all too easy to forget that there is church life outside our own parish. There are times when we get so engrossed in our local concerns that we cease to care about what other churches are doing or about joining with them to share matters of common interest. This attitude is surely wrong, but it is one which is reinforced when there are too few people in any congregation who are prepared to look further afield and to see their service to the Church as happening largely outside their own parish. There are a number of ways in which this may happen, for example in learning or teaching in association with other churches, or in participation in wider church structures.

There are various reasons for doing this. The first may be pure necessity; the majority of churches, for example, do not have sufficient resources to offer their own lay training courses, and if you wish to do something like this you may be put on to a course run by a number of churches together, or by the deanery or diocese. Secondly, you may feel a particular commitment to the ecumenical movement and be led to undertake some form of service in that context, which will inevitably bring you into contact with the other Christian denominations in your area. Thirdly, you may be interested in the structures of the Church 'above' the level of the parish and, in the case of the Church of England, seek election to the Deanery Synod, or else be alert to the practical needs of that or similar inter-parochial bodies. Your diocesan magazine will provide information about needs and activities in your area.

There are many rewards in involvement of this sort. You very soon get to know far more about the wider Church and the churches in your area than you could hope to do from your own local pews. This can be both stimulating and enlightening, as it becomes clear that there are other ways of doing things, as well as different needs and different problems. It is also a good safeguard against narrow-mindedness, as you are made to see that the familiar pattern of church life is neither the only one nor necessarily the best one. For someone who is separated or divorced there is also the great advantage of a fresh start: service is offered and friendships are made on the basis of the person that you now are and not as you are remembered from the past. It is also a way of getting to know, and perhaps help or befriend, Christians from other churches in a similar situation.

Leadership

I have already referred to the vulnerability of divorced Christians who are in a position of leadership within the church. There may also be further complications if this leadership has been one of the factors that led to the breakdown of the marriage in the first place. But whether or not this is the case, the Christian leader will need special support from those around. It is worth adding, too, that while the concern for clergy wives whose marriages break up is most welcome and long overdue, some thought needs to be given to the pastoral care of the clergy themselves who are in this position.

If, however, we assume just such a caring response on the part of those ministered to, there is no reason why divorced Christians who have gifts of leadership (or related teaching or pastoral gifts) should not exercise them within the Church. Some will have a vocation to the ordained ministry and there are at present a number of ordinands in training for the Anglican ministry who have been divorced. Because of the confused attitudes that prevail at the moment in the Church of England the fulfilment of such vocations seems to depend, at least in part, on the subjective views of those in authority. One divorced deaconess told me of the very positive and encouraging attitude adopted by her selection committee (who nonetheless probed into the causes for the marital breakdown) while others were more cynical about the standpoints of particular bishops.

For lay leaders the position is less difficult, although those aspiring to overseas missionary service should be aware that some bishops will refuse to work with people who are divorced. This is an uncomfortable fact of life and, as we shall see in the next chapter, until the Church of England as a whole agrees on and pursues an unambiguous stance on the whole question of divorce and remarriage, there is little that can be done beyond endeavouring to demonstrate one's own integrity.

Lay leadership is a vital area of growth in the Church in the late twentieth century. More and more churches are coming to realize the value of shared leadership and obviously with, in some areas, a shortage of clergy, this is essential if the Church is to survive. Yet there are some churches where even the use of laity to lead prayers and read lessons is discouraged. It is important to remember that any such opposition is likely to be based on a general principle rather than for reasons of marital status.

So, those with gifts of leadership ought to be encouraged to use them. There are an increasing number of training courses available either at diocesan level or arranged by individual churches, and these are important both in developing such gifts and in providing the necessary instruction and guidelines as to their use. The responsibilities, however, are not to be regarded lightly, and may offer a formidable challenge to someone who has been through divorce.

Evangelism

The story of the Woman of Samaria (John 4.1–42) is that of a most unlikely evangelist. Everything was loaded against her. To begin with she was not only a woman, but a Samaritan woman, a member of a breakaway sect of Judaism with whom Jesus, as a Jewish rabbi, ought to have had nothing to do. Furthermore she was not only divorced and remarried – there had been no fewer than five divorces. This unlikely character is used in a variety of ways by Jesus. Firstly, the fact that she is a Samaritan, a member of a minority group, is an opportunity for him to teach on the nature of true worship. Secondly, the woman's background is the subject of Jesus's supernatural knowledge; this gives her some idea of who he is and reveals her belief in the coming of the Messiah. Finally, and most important for our purposes, her testimony is a decisive factor in the conversion of many Samaritans, and it is worth remembering that in this she is working alongside Jesus. Some of her countrymen believe because of what she herself tells them; others believe because she takes them to Jesus to hear for themselves.

This is a story to give new heart and fresh encouragement to anyone whose marriage has not stood the test. This Samaritan woman has a tremendous responsibility laid upon her, following her recognition of the true nature of

Jesus (an insight which seems not to have been shared by his disciples at this stage). Like all natural evangelists she witnesses spontaneously to her own people in their own situations and they respond to her as one of them.

In the same way contemporary secular society may respond readily to a divorced Christian, as both to a familiar face and to a familiar situation. If, therefore, someone who is divorced has gifts of evangelism, which may take a quite modest form – perhaps a desire just to share with others what God has done for him or her – what better incentive can there be to use them?

The opportunities for new directions in the Church, then, are many, if the Church allows us to seek them. It may take some persuasion, and this fact needs to be accepted lovingly and graciously. With God all things are possible, and where there are gifts to be used in his service, sooner or later someone will discern them. Prayer, patience and love will in the end overcome any opposition.

FOR BIBLE READING AND PRAYER
Read Isaiah 40.1–11:

Comfort, comfort my people,
   says your God.
Speak tenderly to Jerusalem,
   and proclaim to her
that her hard service has been completed,
   that her sin has been paid for,
that she has received from the Lord's hand
   double for all her sins.

A voice of one calling:
'In the desert prepare
   the way for the Lord;
make straight in the wilderness
   a highway for our God.

Every valley shall be raised up,
    every mountain and hill made low;
the rough ground shall become level,
    the rugged places a plain.
And the glory of the Lord will be revealed,
    and all mankind together will see it.
    For the mouth of the Lord has spoken.'

A voice says, 'Cry out.'
    And I said, 'What shall I cry?'

'All men are like grass,
    and all their glory is like the flowers of the field.
The grass withers and the flowers fall,
    because the breath of the Lord blows on them.
    Surely the people are grass.
The grass withers and the flowers fall,
    but the word of our God stands for ever.'

O Zion, bringer of good tidings,
    go up on a high mountain.
O Jerusalem, bringer of good tidings,
    lift up your voice with a shout,
lift it up, do not be afraid;
    say to the towns of Judah,
    'Here is your God!'
See, the Sovereign Lord comes with power,
    and his arm rules for him.
See, his reward is with him,
    and his recompense accompanies him.
He tends his flock like a shepherd:
    He gathers the lambs in his arms
    and carries them close to his heart;
    he gently leads those that have young.

In the light of what has been said about the role of a divorced Christian in the church, the three themes of this passage will strike familiar chords.

The first is the message of God's forgiveness. The penalty paid in exile by Israel has been more than enough to atone for her disobedience. Notice that this message is conveyed 'tenderly' – there is nothing grudging about it. Elsewhere the fact of forgiveness is also proclaimed joyfully, cf. Zephaniah 3.14–15: 'Be glad and rejoice with all your heart, O Daughter of Jerusalem! The Lord has taken away your punishment, he has turned back your enemy.'

Secondly, this forgiveness leads on to a twofold obligation. The prophetic voice in the earlier verses calls (symbolically) for the Lord's way to be prepared: there are obstacles to be removed and the implication is that this is going to be hard work. Similarly in the verse about Zion (I have taken the alternative reading here which is thought by many scholars to be the correct one), Zion has to pass the message on to the other towns of Judah; there is an obligation to proclaim the word of God. God's forgiveness, then, brings with it a call to his service, both in speech and action.

Thirdly, there is the theme of reassurance about the nature of God. He is the Sovereign Lord, so there can be no doubt as to the value both of his forgiveness and of his service. But he is also a compassionate shepherd; the God who offers forgiveness tenderly exhibits that same tenderness in his care for his people.

If you read on further in Isaiah 40 you will find repeated the reassurance that God is both Sovereign Creator of all things and the protector of individuals, giving life and strength to the weak:

He gives strength to the weary and increases the power of the weak. Even youths grow tired and weary, and young men stumble and fall, but those who hope in the Lord will renew their strength. They will soar on wings like eagles; they will run and not grow weary, they will walk and not be faint.   (vv. 29–31).

Let us pray for this strength in all that we do in God's service.

Jesus said to his disciples, 'The harvest is plentiful but the workers are few. Ask the Lord of the harvest, therefore, to send out workers into his harvest field' (Matt. 9.37–8).

Lord Jesus, forgive us for the many times that we lose sight of our calling to work for you in your harvest field. Forgive our reticence and clumsiness; above all forgive our preoccupation with ourselves and what we are at the expense of helping to spread the good news of who you are.

We pray that you will show us how we can serve you and that you will give us the courage to use the gifts that you have given us.

And may the God of all grace restore us and make us strong and keep us steadfast, to whom be the power for ever. Amen.

Suggestions for Further Reading

Mowbrays are currently bringing out a series of Parish Handbooks which cover a wide range of church-related topics including youth work, pastoral work, pastoral counselling and lay ministry which can be used as a source of ideas for service as well as guidelines in the exercise of particular ministries. Two other books already referred to may also be of use: John Perry's *Christian Leadership* and David Watson's *I Believe in the Church*.

References

1 D. Phypers, *Christian Marriage in Crisis* (MARC Europe 1985), p.125ff.
2 ibid., p.127.
3 M. Green, *I Believe in Satan's Downfall* (Hodder & Stoughton 1981), pp.247–8.
4 J. Perry, *Christian Leadership* (Hodder & Stoughton 1983), p.113.
5 See, for example, G. Carey, *The Church in the Market Place*, Kingsway Publications 1984).

7

Conclusion: The Church, Divorce and Remarriage

If this book has a single dominant message, it is the plea for more encouragement and better pastoral care to be given to Christians whose marriages have ended. I have several times suggested that to be both a Christian and divorced is something of a paradoxical situation in that the pain of marriage breakdown is a pain which other Christians are often unable or unwilling to help alleviate. It seems to be dawning on some people only very slowly that care for, and acceptance of, the divorced does not constitute a devaluation of the Christian ideal of marriage. And in the case of perhaps the majority of Christians who do show such love and concern their attitudes appear to stand in stark contrast to the official 'hard line' attitude of the Church of England towards both divorce and remarriage.

There is no doubt that the Church of England, in particular, is collectively in a state of confusion on these questions. Strong and conflicting views are held by clergy and laity alike, for which there are theological, historical, ethical and social reasons.

I do not wish to explore these in any depth here, but simply to give a very brief outline of the state of affairs in the Church today, both in theory and in practice, and how this has come about. Those who wish to delve more deeply into such questions should not have any difficulty in obtaining the relevant documents. Although I have not given any consideration to remarriage in this book, it seems appropriate to include it here insofar as the topics of divorce and remarriage have normally been treated together in the various reports and debates initiated by the Church.

One further point. In the course of writing this book I have met and talked with quite a few clergy who have been divorced, some of whom have also remarried. Theirs is a unique situation in the Church and one which I do not propose to examine now. I would only say that I have been struck again and again by the love and understanding shown by these men for their fellow Christians, often in the face of extreme hurt inflicted on them by those in authority in particular. They deserve at least as much love and support from the rest of us in return.

Conflicts in the Church of England

Indissolubility

The Church of England seems to have been doomed almost from the outset to turmoil and confusion over divorce and remarriage. On the one hand it is torn – as all Christians must be – between a desire to uphold the ideal of marriage and feelings of compassion towards those who in reality are trapped in a loveless and unhappy union. Additionally, however, it is caught up in conflicts between Church and State where, for example, the civil law grants clergy the right to remarry divorcees in church while the ecclesiastical authorities actively discourage their exercising this right.

The doctrine of the indissolubility of marriage was absorbed by the Church of England at the time of the Reformation. It holds that there is no way in which man can 'put asunder' those whom God has joined together. If a marriage proves intolerable to one or both partners the only way out has been separation 'from bed and board', with no possibility of remarriage during the partner's lifetime.

This doctrine, associated above all with Roman Catholicism, has tended to obscure the gap between the ideal and the reality of many marriages over the years, not least because of the nature of the 'way round it'. It is not admitted that there can be problems within marriage that are so great warrant separation. Instead, if a marriage that is held to be 'indissoluble' breaks down, then the response is to try to prove that there was never any marriage bond in the first place. The concept of nullity has been used and abused (particularly by the Church of Rome) for hundreds of years and is still being extended to cover more and more possibilities at the present time.

English Divorce Legislation

Among the Protestant churches the position of the Church of England on divorce and remarriage contrasts the most radically with the situation in English law. The tension between Church and State on this issue goes back to the 1857 Divorce Act, and the subsequent legislation of 1937 and 1971 has widened the gap further. This division relates not only to the procedures of divorce and remarriage (both of them straightforward in law but regarded in a very different light by the Church), but also to the role of Anglican clergy and the use of their churches in the remarriage of divorcees. Consequently the Church of England as the established Church is often in the position of refusing a religious ceremony to those whom the law of the land freely permits to marry.

Before the 1857 Divorce Act there had been no provision for divorce except by Act of Parliament or on the grounds of nullity, a process open only to the rich or influential. This Act allowed a husband to divorce his wife on the grounds of her adultery (cf. Matt. 5.32) and also transferred questions of divorce from ecclesiastical to civic jurisdiction. At the same time clergy were given the legal power to remarry people who had been divorced under these circumstances. The reaction of the Church, however, was to turn this round and make it clear that the clergy were under no obligation to use this power. This attitude has prevailed ever since, as successive Convocations have urged clergy to use their discretion negatively, which is almost tantamount to forbidding the practice. An Anglican clergyman wishing to exercise his legal right still needs to think carefully before doing so.

The grounds for divorce and nullity were considerably extended under the 1937 Matrimonial Clauses Act, for women as well as men. In 1969, as is well known, the Divorce Reform Act took the significant step of abolishing the idea of guilty and innocent parties (and the notion of a 'matrimonial offence') and substituting the concept of the irretrievable breakdown of marriage (on one of five counts) as the only grounds for divorce. It is interesting that this was earlier advocated in a report commissioned by the then Archbishop of Canterbury, entitled *Putting Asunder*.[1] Yet the authors of that report held that they were considering the law as it stood in secular society, not the discipline of the Church. There was therefore the unfortunate implication that a more humane approach to divorce might be denied to Anglican Christians.

The result of the 1969 Act, which became operational in 1971, has undoubtedly been a huge increase in the incidence of divorce which can only be attributed to the easier procedure. The same holds true for the number of remarriages, and current figures also show the *re*divorce figures standing at about one-fifth of the divorce rate. These sorry statistics have in their turn, it seems, led to a polarizing of attitudes within the Church of England on the question of both divorce and remarriage. This, as we shall see below, has given rise to a confusing variation in practice as far as remarriage is concerned, as well as the status in the Church of those who are divorced.

The Situation Today

The Biblical Position

The Church's stance on divorce has been further complicated by developments in modern biblical scholarship. The relevant biblical material is clearly set out and summarized in David Atkinson's *To Have and to Hold*.[2] The author concludes that both the Old and New Testaments affirm God's law for the permanence of marriage, but that there is also a need to legislate for the exceptions that are due to the 'hardness of men's hearts'. He adds that when divorce occurs the marriage bond is completely dissolved and remarriage can be presupposed.

Some scholars, however, have questioned the validity of the two main passages in the New Testament which appear to sanction divorce in certain circumstances. The first is the so-called 'Matthean exception', where 'marital unfaithfulness' on the part of the wife is the one possibility for divorce admitted by Jesus (Matt. 5.32 and 19.9ff). Some writers maintain that this is a late addition, representing a concession by the early Church to social reality, while others question the meaning of the Greek word *porneia* (traditionally translated as 'adultery') and argue that it has a more general meaning of sexual immorality.

The other New Testament passage usually quoted in these debates is the 'Pauline privilege' (1 Cor. 7.15) where divorce is said to be permissible if one partner who is not a Christian leaves the home of his or her own accord. Some scholars have argued that this passage sanctions separation only, not divorce (which is also a possible interpretation of Matt. 19), while others see it as allowing both divorce and remarriage in this particular extreme situation.

The exegetical arguments are of course much more detailed and refined than I have made them appear here. But even the gist of such debates should be sufficient to indicate how biblical arguments can be used to quite different effect and may tend, therefore, to add to the confusion in the Church of England rather than resolve it.

Discrepancies within the Church of England

I have already suggested that some of the confused thinking

within the Anglican Church stems, on the one hand, from the desire of the established Church to uphold a certain moral standard against the prevailing trends in secular society and, on the other, from a natural impulse to regard with compassion those whose marriages have failed. It seems that this problem defies resolution for several reasons. Atkinson, for example, argues persuasively that making divorce as difficult as possible is not the way to uphold and strengthen the Christian view of marriage.[3] Then there are the divisions within the Church itself. I would go so far as to say that the existence of different styles of churchmanship within the Church of England, which we tend to regard rather benignly, can be a very real obstacle to the average Christian in the pew when he has to sort out matters of great personal importance to him in the face of completely opposing views from those in authority.

It would be both wrong and divisive to attempt to base any conclusions on impressions that are inevitably general and subjective. Let us simply note the uneasy cohabitation of two opposite points of view within the Church of England. At one extreme there seems to be a clear desire on the part of some Anglo-Catholics not to follow any path that would distance them from the Roman Catholic Church. So, where divorce and remarriage are concerned, divorce can only be possible as a result of nullity (or an extension of that idea), and remarriage otherwise unacceptable. Anglo-Catholic clergy might be expected to exercise their right of conscience not to remarry divorcees nor to allow their churches to be used for that purpose.

The opposite tendency is to follow the practice of the Free Churches who generally admit divorce and remarriage (subject to certain pastoral considerations) on the basis of the biblical passages mentioned earlier. Yet the scripturally-based approach also gives rise to a 'hard line' attitude amongst those who interpret the Bible as saying that remarriage for any reason is adulterous.[4]

Between these two positions there is further variation in

belief and practice in the churches today. At the local level, much may depend on the attitude of the bishop, who may use his discretion, for example, to refuse to license a divorced person as a lay reader or not allow a divorcee to go forward for ordination training. The local clergy may decide to exclude someone from Holy Communion for a time, or may refuse permission to a divorced priest to celebrate in their churches.

In March 1986 the *Birmingham Diocesan Bulletin* reported the outcome of the Bishop's request for information regarding remarriage in church. Out of the 176 respondents there were 70 parishes where remarriages had taken place and 74 where this had been refused (and, presumably, 32 where it had not been requested or followed up). Overall, only 251 remarriages out of 917 requests were actually solemnized, less than 10 per cent of the total number of marriages solomnized in the diocese for the period in question. Now it seems likely that figures such as these would vary a great deal from one diocese to another, for social and economic reasons as well as spiritual ones, so it is not really possible to draw any conclusions from this survey without further information. A further variation would surely also be found in the type of service offered to those seeking remarriage, ranging from a traditional order of marriage to a service of blessing which might be modelled on the marriage service or specially devised for the occasion.

The way forward for the Church of England is far from clear. In 1981 the General Synod passed a motion that included the assertion that there were circumstances in which a divorced person might be married in church during the lifetime of a former partner. The Standing Committee were asked to prepare a report setting out possible procedures for such cases, but their proposals were eventually rejected by the diocesan synods.

The remarriage question is a complex one. It seems to me likely that the Church of England will in due course thrash out a set of procedures for remarriage in church, but I find it hard to be optimistic about the degree of uniformity with which they might be applied. In the meantime, however, it is not too much to hope that the debates on remarriage may produce a greater awareness of the spiritual and pastoral needs of the separated, divorced and remarried people within our churches. I pray that this book may be a small contribution to such an understanding.

FOR BIBLE READING AND PRAYER
Twice in the Gospels we read that Jesus had compassion on the crowds following him because they were 'like sheep without a shepherd' (Mark 6.34). In Matthew's version the crowds are described as 'harassed and helpless' (Matt. 9.36). In this concluding chapter we have focused attention particularly on the Church and therefore on those concerned with its doctrine and discipline. These are the shepherds who have a special responsibility for offering guidance to their sheep as well as caring for them in other ways. And it is important to remember that the model for our Christian leaders today is Christ himself who does more than ask our obedience – he gives us his compassion.

Read John 21.15–19:

When they had finished eating, Jesus said to Simon Peter, 'Simon son of John, do you truly love me more than these?'
   'Yes, Lord,' he said, 'you know that I love you'.
   Jesus said, 'Feed my lambs.'
   Again Jesus said, 'Simon son of John, do you truly love me?'
   He answered, 'Yes, Lord, you know that I love you.'
   Jesus said, 'Take care of my sheep.'
   The third time he said to him, 'Simon son of John, do you love me?'
   Peter was hurt because Jesus asked him the third time, 'Do

you love me?' He said, 'Lord, you know all things; you know that I love you.'

Jesus said, 'Feed my sheep. I tell you the truth, when you were younger you dressed yourself and went where you wanted; but when you are old you will stretch out your hands, and someone else will dress you and lead you where you do not want to go.' Jesus said this to indicate the kind of death by which Peter would glorify God. Then he said to him, 'Follow me!'

The story of Peter before the events of Easter and Pentecost bears a great deal of resemblance to our own experience in the Christian life. He was a man who was filled with enthusiasm when things were going well, and his failure when they were not rings bells with all of us. Peter could not cope with the threats and taunts of those who did not share his beliefs, nor could he understand Jesus's love and concern for those outsiders. And it is not unreasonable to suppose that for Peter, as for the other disciples, the belief that Jesus was the Messiah and the sight of him being taken off to die a criminal's death must have been virtually irreconcilable.

This was the man to whom Jesus gave a particular responsibility: 'Feed my lambs . . . take care of my sheep.' Our Christian leaders are no less fallible than Peter was; there will be times when collectively or individually they will apparently fail to hear or to obey the promptings of the Spirit; they may lack compassion, wisdom, understanding or courage. Yet we should not forget that they are there because Jesus has called them and that they, like Peter, will be hurt if we doubt their love for him.

If you are an 'ordinary Christian in the pew' (if such a stereotype actually exists) pray for your pastors and leaders. Not just for those you know, who care for you and your local church, but for those who are more remote: the men and women who have to grapple with theological and doctrinal questions and guide others in the everyday application of abstract principles. Pray that they will remain faithful to Christ's commands to Peter. And if any such people happen to be reading this book, then you will not need me to ask you to pray for those whose lives are directly affected by your work, for it will in any case weigh constantly on your hearts and minds.

This passage also deals with the consequences of Peter's obedience, for it is generally taken to be a prediction of martyrdom by crucifixion. However, the last two verses have also a more general application which provides an appropriate point for us to end with. This is the call to discipleship which goes out not just to the shepherds but to the rest of us as well, the sheep. Our obedience to that call may well mean that we are led where we do not want to go. But, when we commit ourselves completely and whole-heartedly, we have here the assurance that in so doing we are glorifying God.

If it seems hard at times to obey this command, 'Follow me', remember that it is not the Shepherd but the other sheep who make things difficult for us. It is not God's will that the Christian life should be unalleviated gloom, how-ever character-building some people may feel this to be. So let us fix our hearts and minds on God and pray for the gifts of his Holy Spirit – for love, joy and peace in our hearts. When we do this, whatever our individual circumstances, we can surely claim (in the words of the old Beatles' song) 'we can work it out!'

Jesus told his disciples: 'Remain in my love . . . I have told you this so that my joy may be in you and that your joy may be complete. My command is this: Love each other as I have loved you' (John 15.9, 11–12).

Almighty God, whose Son restored Mary Magdalen to health of mind and body and called her to be a witness to his resurrection: forgive us and heal us by your grace, that we may serve you in the power of his risen life; who is

alive and reigns with you and the Holy Spirit, one God, now and for ever. Amen.
(*The Collect for St Mary Magdalen, ASB 1980, and adopted particularly by the Magdalene Fellowship*).

Suggestions for further reading
K. Kelly, *Divorce and Second Marriage: Facing the Challenge* (Collins 1982), looks at the question of indissolubility and treats various pastoral questions. David Atkinson's *To Have and to Hold* (Collins 1979) is highly recommended and has a very full bibliography for further reading. Some idea of the doctrinal issues involved can be gained from one of the Church of England reports on marriage and divorce; e.g. *Marriage, Divorce and the Church* (SPCK 1972) sets out the problem in straightforward terms. On legal questions a book such as F.E. Mostyn, *Marriage and the Law* (Oyez Publishing 1976), is a readable guide to all aspects of the subject.

References
1 SPCK 1966.
2 D. Atkinson, *To Have and to Hold* (Collins 1979) see especially chapter 4.
3 ibid., p.191.
4 See, for example, W.A. Heth, and G.A. Wenham *Jesus and Divorce* (Hodder & Stoughton 1984).

Appendix

1. *Social Security, Income Tax, National Insurance Leaflets issued by the Department of Health and Social Security, which are available free at their offices, public libraries, some post offices, etc., include:*

NI 95 National Insurance Guide for Divorced Women
NP.32A Your Retirement Pension if You are Widowed or Divorced
FB.3 Help for One-Parent Families
SB.1 Cash Help (claiming supplementary benefit if you are bringing up children on your own or only able to work part time).

If you are considering becoming self-employed, see:

NI 41 National Insurance Guide for the Self-employed
IR 28 Starting a New Business
IR 56 Tax: Employed or Self-employed

(the last two available from the Inland Revenue).

2. *Some Addresses*

Secular bodies

Divorce Conciliation Advisory Service, 38 Ebury Street, London SW1 (offers crisis counselling and longer-term counselling for those in the process of separation or divorce).

Gingerbread, 35 Wellington Street, London WC2 (self-help for one-parent families).

Mediation in Divorce, 51 Sheen Road, Richmond, Surrey.

National Council for One-Parent Families, 255 Kentish Town Road, London NW5 2LX.

Parents Anonymous, 49 Godstone Road, Purley, Surrey (also has a number of local branches listed in the Phone Book under P).

Solicitors Family Law Association, 154 Fleet Street, London EC4A 2HZ (its members are committed to pursuing an amicable approach to divorce).

Christian Organizations

Lee Abbey, Lynton, Devon EX35 6JJ (a Christian community, conference and holiday centre, which includes in its programme a special week for one-parent families).

The Magdalene Fellowship, c/o 45 Wallingford Street, Wantage, Oxon OX12 8AV (seeks to draw into fellowship those who have been hurt by society or even felt rejected in Christian circles because they are divorced, separated or remarried).

Training Courses

Care and Counsel, Mary Magdalene Church, Holloway Road, London N7 (arranges short courses and seminars in counselling, etc.).

Wholeness through Christ, 8 Beaulieu Way, Swanwick, Derbyshire DE55 1DR (biblical counselling method).

Westminster Pastoral Foundation, 23 Kensington Square, London W8 5HN (for training and supervision of counsellors).

Your local diocesan offices should be able to provide details of lay training schemes operating in your area.